At Home Within

A Practical Christian Guide to Creating
Peace, Order and Beauty at Home

MAYA MURPHY

At Home Within © Copyright 2026 Maya Murphy

All rights reserved. No part of this publication may be reproduced, distributed or transmitted in any form or by any means, including photocopying, recording, or other electronic or mechanical methods, without the prior written permission of the publisher, except in the case of brief quotations embodied in critical reviews and certain other noncommercial uses permitted by copyright law.

Although the author and publisher have made every effort to ensure that the information in this book was correct at press time, the author and publisher do not assume and hereby disclaim any liability to any party for any loss, damage, or disruption caused by errors or omissions, whether such errors or omissions result from negligence, accident, or any other cause.

Adherence to all applicable laws and regulations, including international, federal, state and local governing professional licensing, business practices, advertising, and all other aspects of doing business in the US, Canada or any other jurisdiction is the sole responsibility of the reader and consumer.

Scripture taken from the HOLY BIBLE, NEW INTERNATIONAL VERSION®. Copyright © 1973, 1978, 1984 by International Bible Society. Used by permission of Zondervan. All rights reserved.

Neither the author nor the publisher assumes any responsibility or liability whatsoever on behalf of the consumer or reader of this material. Any perceived slight of any individual or organization is purely unintentional.

The resources in this book are provided for informational purposes only and should not be used to replace the specialized training and professional judgment of a health care or mental health care professional.

Neither the author nor the publisher can be held responsible for the use of the information provided within this book. Please always consult a trained professional before making any decision regarding treatment of yourself or others.

ISBN: 979-8-90057-221-5 - Ebook

ISBN: 979-8-90057-222-2 - Paperback

ISBN: 979-8-90057-223-9 - Hardcover

Get Your Free Gift!

To get the best experience with this book, I've found readers who download and use The Video Summary can implement faster and take the next steps needed to create a home they love to be in.

VIDEO SUMMARY

Want a video summary of this book that will help you start making progress on **YOUR** home quickly?

Check out this video training and overview of the process.

In this training I cover how to make your home:

1. **Personal** - Create a Space that feels like you
2. **Serve you** - Create Order and Systems
3. **Beautiful to You** - Get your Home to look "right"

ATHOMEWITHIN.ORG

You can get a copy by visiting:

AtHomeWithin.org

This book is dedicated to my first love, the reason for my existence, and the essence within me, Jesus Christ. He has shown through His example that He not only meets every eternal and unseen need within us, He also meets our physical needs. He made us as human beings uniquely as both spiritual and physical beings, so He inspired this book that blends both of those aspects together in the spaces that we get to dwell in. He knows every hair on our head and every breadcrumb in our homes. He has helped fill my home with all that makes life sweet until I'm home forever with Him one day.

Contents

Chapter 1:   Laying the Foundation Within Us 5

Chapter 2:   Clearing the Ground................................23

Chapter 3:   The Space that Serves You................................53

Chapter 4:   Planning Your Resources................................75

Chapter 5:   All that You Need and Nothing You Don't 99

Chapter 6:   Tiny Powerhouse Routines 121

Chapter 7:   Renovations and Remodels 131

Chapter 8:   Design Simplified 157

Chapter 9:   Bringing it All Together 185

Appendix A: Personal Monthly Budget Template 197

Appendix B: Personal Renovation Budget Template 201

About the Author 205

Acknowledgements................................207

Introduction

Do messes, clutter, imperfections, chores to be done, expectations, or broken design rules ever rob you of your peace in your home? Do you ever apologize for your house or feel uncomfortable allowing guests you care about in? Does it ever seem like your house isn't good enough? Have you ever felt like "Home" is this distant and maybe even unattainable goal for the future, instead of settling into what God has given you to be your home on Earth today and letting it serve you? Has the clutter in your mind ever spilled over into your spaces and become overwhelming? Have you ever thought, "Where do I even start?"

What I learned by working through some of those struggles in my own life, as well as renovating houses into beautiful homes for others to live in, is that making a home is more than making a house pretty. It doesn't have to be perfect, and it can actually be fun. I learned that even without professional experience, you can turn your space into a beautiful home that reflects who you are, recharges you, and fills you up. Gaining the right knowledge and perspective is all it takes. This book serves as your guide, offering practical steps and a streamlined path to creating the home of your dreams.

For me, first and foremost, that means looking up. I invite you to put on the glasses of an eternal perspective as the lens through which you view the other aspects of your home and space. Remember our perfect God loves each of us deeply, even in the middle of any and every mess, and He cares about not just our spiritual side but our physical one as well. And we are made for joy today! Remembering this truth allows us to love ourselves and each other so that it oozes out of the walls. A house can be functional and beautiful, and when we add these intangibles, then it's a home.

My husband, Dave, and I started playing grown-up monopoly together in 2007, buying houses, renovating, and turning them into beautiful homes for other people, mainly offering them as rent-to-own. This meant that the residents living in them could rent the home until they were ready to buy it and could also start to make the home their own. In the meantime, we were renting on an Air Force Base and were quite content. Then when we bought our own home to live in, our 20th remodel began, and the first one for us. I found the process of creating a sacred, personal, beautiful space for me and my family so inspiring that I decided to write this book to share it with you. The process has challenged me, made me grow in intentionality, and caused me to think more deeply about what our spaces mean and what I want them to mean. Along the way, I've learned what questions to ask, tools to snap out of it if I get stuck in old thoughts, and how to give myself permission in many new ways. On a practical side, we've also learned how to help a home function well, some design tips that make a space feel better to be in, how to work well as a team, and how to plan out resources because it's hard to feel at home when your house is stressing you out financially. Those insights and more are shared with you here. Now our home serves us and our guests so that it's grounding, liberating, rooted in faith, and beautiful. And in the moments when I forget, it's a much faster path back to peace.

This book is for anyone who wants to be comfortable in their space, to feel like they can kick off their shoes and their worries and just be. This is more than just about design and pretty pictures because that's only a piece of home.

This is so you can have that space in the world that feels good to be in; a place where you can play to your heart's content; a space that feels like you, that serves you, and that is quite simply home.

This is an actionable book.

Together, we'll go through foundational elements of understanding your values and then creating a space that supports the habits and routines that align with those values. This will give clarity on what you want and don't want in your home so that it serves you and the people living in it. Then we'll talk about resources, making sure that the work you choose to do fits within the time and money that works in each season of life.

This leads into the functionality of your home. How do you take care of your space so that it has a flow? You'll learn some easy habits and hacks to get your home working well for you. How do you set it up so that it makes sense with the activities you want to do there? You'll also learn where to invest in unseen items that help a home function behind the scenes.

Then we'll talk about beauty. A mountain landscape is beautiful all year round, even when the flowers aren't in bloom. In the same way, a home that serves the people who live in it and come to it, that has everything you need to thrive and nothing you don't, is beautiful in each season of life. You'll also learn some design elements that help pull a space together. Sometimes the way to make a space feel right is quite simply with metals that look good together, colors that are not under or overwhelming, and pictures hung at a good height, for example.

Why make our living spaces a home? Our homes shape us more than we often realize. Home isn't just where we live, it's what we live inside of every day. The atmosphere, the order (or chaos), the beauty (or neglect)... it quietly forms your mood, your habits, your patience, and even your ability to rest. A home isn't a luxury; it's a foundation. Making your space a home is one of the most practical ways to cooperate with peace - and to create room for it to stay. When your space is functional and cared for, it gives back: more energy, more clarity, more margin and more joy. This isn't about perfection. It's about support.

Let's create homes where we can recharge to be ready to do the work God has put us on Earth to do. When we do this, our everyday homes become one of the happiest places on Earth. You hold the keys in your hands, and all you have to do is keep turning the pages.

Chapter 1

Laying the Foundation Within Us

"You should live the best life you can," said my wise friend Joe, who humbly lives a remarkable life. Joe is rooted in his faith, and from that foundation has confidently and courageously pursued two fruitful careers. He also invented a piece of equipment that has led to his financial wealth, balanced hobbies, and family life, and even worked as an actor on the side. With a warm side hug, he added, "That's why you should remodel your kitchen—to create a space that nurtures you and your loved ones. When you walk into a home that reflects who you truly are, you feel grounded. This isn't about competition or impressing others; it's about generosity—offering your best self to your family first."

Joe's words echoed as I looked around the "perfect" kitchen we'd created. As we fill our homes with meaningful pieces, both old and new, we cultivate a sanctuary that resonates with our values and experiences. This journey is about creating a space that invites warmth, love, and connection—a true home where we can all thrive.

This chapter is filled with stories, each teaching a foundational element of home. It can be easier to glean these lessons from a story than a phrase, just like Jesus taught in parables. We can ponder them in our hearts, learn from them, and build on them.

You can't buy "home." Believe me, I've tried. My husband and I have tried sparing no expense, getting the most lavish appliances, the custom cabinets, the custom couches... and what we've found is that there is always one more upgrade that can be done. That search for home in the wrong way was exhausting and left us serving our house. Instead of feeling like we could relax and just be, we were constantly working toward the next item on the house to-do list. Yet when we accomplished it, we only briefly enjoyed it before rushing off to start the next project that would hopefully finally create "home." It felt like we were trying to prove ourselves and that it wasn't good enough. Yet those ideas were just thoughts that we were making up in our minds.

This can become a never-ending sinkhole: even once we've checked off every upgrade on our list, if we still believe that we can buy home, then we'll make one up or move to a more expensive house, forever chasing the feeling of home that we long for in our souls and finding it elusive, slipping through our fingers as we bend our brows, toil, and sweat for the peace we desire between our walls.

Ultimately, that perfect home we long for is heaven, where we get to be in unity with love itself because God is love. The more we bring Him into our homes here on Earth, the more we fill them with love and unity, peace and joy, and the truth of who we are to Him, the more we will get to experience glimpses of the divine home here and now. There are practical ways to bring the beauty of the unseen into our homes, and we'll go through those exercises and strategies in these pages.

Home is just as much about the things you can't see as the things you can. That's why we'll cover both, starting with the inner work.

Intangibles of Home—Love, Acceptance and Connection

In the movie *Greater*, there's a scene where Brandon has just made it to the NFL and signed a lucrative contract. His college teammates say now that he's made it big, he won't have time for them and will be living the high life. Brandon tells them he misses his home. He says that when he's not playing professional football, if they want to find him, they should look in that old house on Cherry Street, the home he grew up in. His mama didn't have the money to make it fancy, but she sure loved her boy, accepted him, cared for him, and made him feel welcome. At the end of the day, when Brandon had enough to afford being anywhere, that's where he chose to be—in that little old house filled with love. This is because he understands that home is about emotional safety and not material perfection. The emotional safety was so profound that even NFL money couldn't buy what Brandon had: a home filled with love.

This is the kind of home my friend Judie Quayle grew up in. Her dad was a carpenter with a modest paycheck. Mom knew how to stretch that income and always said how proud she was of him as a provider. He built the custom, solid wood furniture in the home with such devotion. They lived "wealthy" lives not by having lots of money, but by being diligent with what they had and putting the hard work in toward their home. He dug the pool himself, so they had the luxuries of the rich and earned them through hard labor. Their example shows that home is attainable for all of us, regardless of income levels.

The dinner table was filled with laughter as they each shared stories of the dumbest mistakes they had made that day. In the summer, after dinner, they left the table without cleaning it up and would play games in the backyard to decide who had to do the dishes. Whoever lost did them all! More than the lovely, handmade wooden furnishings undoubtedly were the welcoming spirit, love of family, and ability to not take themselves too seriously. At one point, when they weren't all there, someone walked in and said, "You can just feel the love here!" Even without all the family in it, the love for the home and for each other oozed out of the walls. Judie's parents lived in that home for over 60 years. The home became part of the family.

Connection is a choice. For a while, I had a cute, metal bistro table in the front room of our home that, to me, made that room feel like a Texas front porch. It was simple and quaint, and we would sometimes sit together while we sipped coffee there. The problem was my husband, Dave, had made it clear that he did not like that table. He doesn't state his opinion about that many items, yet I had ignored it because I liked the table and didn't want to do the work of coming up with another idea for that space.

The turning point for me came when I thought about that space from my husband's perspective. He works hard to have this home, yet every time he walks in the door, the front room has a table that he doesn't like, that's not his style, that bugs him a little. I don't want that for him! I want this to feel like home to him too and for him to enjoy it. I realized that I'd been choosing a silly metal table over my own husband. Once I realized that I was prioritizing décor over Dave, the choice became obvious. I decided to let the table go.

After that, we started getting better at honing in on what we each liked. And then the magic happened as we started being able to create together a home that we both liked, a home that was a reflection of both of us together. I came to appreciate and enjoy seeing Dave in our home choices.

Most of the time, Dave was pretty neutral about home choices, and I would get to pick what I wanted. For that reason, when he did show a preference, especially a strong one, I was motivated to honor it.

Not every choice has to be a perfect unity of both of us. In the garage, Dave has a domain. I've told him I don't have authority there. He still may ask my opinion, but he doesn't have to. In other areas, there are times when he tells me he doesn't have a preference, and I just choose. The important mental shift was the priority: Dave is more important than any of the stuff in our home. Like most simple truths, when they are said out loud, they are obvious. Yet before we say them, they can be easily missed as we go about our day-to-day lives and make decisions that seem so important at the time. How this looks for each relationship may be different, but the priority can be the same. The closer Dave and I become, the more our shared space feels like home.

When I was younger and living alone, the more comfortable I felt with myself, the more I felt at home. The more I gave myself permission to slow down, be satisfied, and take a minute to breathe, the more comfortable I became at home. One of my favorite home memories from that season of life was lying on the couch reading a great book series. That was a rare moment in that busy, fluttery season for me to just be instead of running from one place to the next. God finds us in the quiet moments, like a gentle breeze against our cheeks, and refreshes our souls. That connection is what recharges us. It's hard to feel at home when you feel like you should always be focused on the next task. Connection happens in the present moment.

Comfort

A Pinterest-worthy house won't feel like home if you're not comfortable in the space. Home is the ultimate comfort zone, the place where we get to be ourselves, recharge, and prepare to take on the world again. Often, this comfort can come through the consistency and clarity of knowing what to expect, both from a space and the people in it.

My grandma and grandpa's home offered the comfort of consistency. Even now, decades later, I remember fondly the pictures from grandkids taped up on the back of that one hallway door, which was propped open with the oatmeal container full of plastic bead necklaces for grandkids to try on. The routines were comforting too. I still remember the buttered rice that

Grandma served with every lunch and dinner and how we got to pick a Little Debbie dessert after the meal.

They found ways to make their home what everyone wanted, even when it seemed impossible. My clever grandma hung a curtain in my Daddy's basement bedroom when he was a kid (even though there was no window) because he really wanted a window in his room. Every time I went down to that room and saw that little curtain, I had to pull it back and look at the wood siding beneath the curtain that matched the siding everywhere else in the room. Even as a kid, I chuckled and marveled at her creativity. Sometimes the best solutions are the unexpected (and often imperfect) ones.

Grandma and Grandpa's house was a home. We could always count on Grandma and Grandpa's house being the same each time we came back. It wasn't the perfection but the familiarity and the order that made their space feel so good.

Grandma's house didn't change just for the sake of changing. Change can be good, but new doesn't necessarily mean better. Some items that aren't new are irreplaceable and valuable in a way that a brand-new item cannot be. Just like the Mona Lisa, the Louvre, the Eiffel Tower, the Pyramids, and other treasures of the world that would not be improved with something new, old furnishings anchor us and can have strong memories, meaning, and history that keep our hearts and homes grounded.

Clarity may be the greater depth of what Grandma's home offered. I knew what to expect; I knew the boundaries (even though they were almost entirely unspoken), where to find items, and what chair Grandma and Grandpa would sit in. As human beings, clarity feels safe because we know what to expect and what is expected of us.

Another good example comes from my friend Jane. When Jane's grandmother died, there was one item she said she wanted. It was a painting that hung in the dining room of her grandmother's home, one she had seen since her childhood, and one that now continues to hang in Jane's dining room. This opens the doors for stories and conversations that pass their family legacy. And when we make it important, when we share our heritage with our children and those we love, doesn't that also teach them the irreplaceable value of our roots? Doesn't it help them discover who they are by learning where they came from? Let's slow down enough to look around at the treasures that may be right under our noses before we rush out and fill the walls with something new.

Authenticity and Conviction

As my cheerful, Southern friend Brandy unapologetically says, "I like what I like!" With all the voices and marketing trying to tell us what we want, how do we stay true to ourselves like Brandy? Here's a story that sets a good example.

Nori, my cousin and designer who helped us for eight years to design and renovate homes, worked at a countertop and cabinet company for over a year. She watched customers come in who would say they wanted a certain style or type of countertop, and over and over again, with the same pitch, she watched the owner convince them that what they really wanted was something else. He would tell them about the durability; he would tell them about current styles and trends. In particular, he often steered clients away from marble, saying it aged, scratched, and stained more easily than some of the modern options like quartz. The majority of folks ended up ordering exactly what he suggested, whether it actually fit their style or not.

Then there was this one woman who came into the store. He gave her the same pitch that he told everyone else, touting the durability of the modern countertops. She listened and left. Several days later, she came back with her head held high. She said she had thought about it and that, yes, she was sure she wanted the marble. She said she understood it's not as durable, she understood it can scratch, and she understands it can show its age over the years. She said all of those features give it character, that she thinks marble ages well, and that it is, in fact, the style she wants. This is what she wants in her home.

In all that time and with all those customers, this particular woman stood out. She made her decision from a place of conviction. She had confidence in her choice. I'd like to see her home. Wouldn't you imagine it to be lovely?

Interestingly enough, we often talk about the durability of kitchen counters, for example, arguing that we need quartz instead of marble because it needs to be durable enough to withstand indoor use for 10 or 20 years. Yet, the Taj Mahal was built hundreds of years ago out of white marble and still stands. Yes, durability matters, but so does soul. Perspective is powerful! So, whatever it is that tugs at your heart, feel free to honor it, feel free to challenge the status quo, and feel free to create a home that is your own Taj Mahal.

We can lean into that side. We can remember how good it feels to be confident and content. We can use that mentality when we have the next decision to make. Like any muscle, the more I practice being in that state, the easier it gets. For the other times, grace abounds.

The times when I've been bold and gone for it, especially when I decided from the gut, I've loved it. The couple of places in our home where I played it safe are still good, even if they're not what they could have been. I accept that and love our home as it is without guilt, but we get one life to live. We might as well live all out!

Hospitality

I first had to learn how to be comfortable in my own home before I was ready to share that space with guests. For a few months, I just worked on making our home comfortable for me and my family, without being clouded by other people or considering what they would think. After I was done making it right for us, adding in guests and hospitality flowed naturally.

What is hospitality? Myspiritualgifts.com says, "Those with this gift [of hospitality] have a natural inclination to warmly welcome and care for others, creating a welcoming environment and meeting both physical and emotional needs." There's value in knowing that this is a gift of the Holy Spirit so that we do not compare our hospitality to others. At the same time, in Romans 12:13, the Apostle Paul encourages believers to be ready to help each other and to practice hospitality. What a good use of the word practice! This is a skill we can develop, and we can learn from each other's hospitality.

I learned from my uncle Jerry and aunt Anne's hospitality. After dinner, Uncle Jerry showed us the extra blankets in the closet and where to find a nightlight if we wanted one. He put himself in our shoes and thought through what needs may arise.

We felt that again when we stayed with Mary Beth in her beautiful home. Her guest room had the WiFi password on a cute little tabletop chalkboard, bath robes and slippers in the closet, and a small basket of toiletries. Remembering how good it felt to be welcomed into her home with that thoughtfulness motivated me to do something for those we love who would make the effort to visit us. What a gift to have someone we care about visit our home.

So, we now have a card displayed in the guest room with our Wi-Fi information and show our guests how to adjust the A/C before they go to bed. We made our guest bathroom nice as a gift to our guests. We made it beautiful to bring nature into our home, the beauty of God's creation, in a creative way, because as finite as we are, what a privilege that our Creator made us in His image with the desire and ability to create as well.

Welcome

My friend Joei told me a helpful story about her childhood friend's home. "It was a safe place," she said. I asked what made it safe, curious about how to create that for others. "Her mom cared about us. She would ask how I was doing and genuinely wanted to know the answer." Along with some snacks, her mom met their emotional needs. And that little seed was enough to make a lasting impact on a now grown, beautiful woman.

Remember too that people come to our homes to be with us. They're here to step into our lives and world for this little bit of time because we mean something to them. It is a gift when we curl up on the couch with a friend and just be. There's a beautiful vulnerability in letting someone into our sacred spaces of home because it's inviting them into our lives in a physical way. One of my favorite activities as a guest is to peek at the pictures that are up, especially the "outdated" ones that offer a glimpse into past adventures or moments. Our homes are reflections of who we are, which is what makes them uniquely ours.

This is what makes it a gift of hospitality—serving people and welcoming them into our lives. Jesus was welcomed into people's homes, setting an example for us. When we see Jesus in each person, then we see the heart of hospitality, which is ultimately a gift to God through loving others.

Simplicity

We recently went on a family vacation that reminded me once more of the truth in a sign we have posted at home that says, "We must have adventures to know where we truly belong." We stayed in a simple wood camping cabin that was basically a glorified tough shed with a mini fridge, microwave, a queen bed, a couple of loft beds, a plug-in heater, and an A/C unit, along with a wood front patio added on. The community bathrooms were just down the way, and the cute windows were not entirely free of a few harmless bugs. When we realized how rugged these cabins were, we almost canceled the trip, but we'd told the kids we were going, and Dave had a gut feeling we should go.

As we pulled up to the quaint cabins near a small river with sweeping canyon views, without a second thought, I said, "We're home!" And we were. I was surprised at how much it felt like home because of its refreshing simplicity. That little cabin told us we could come as we are. It said we're good enough and don't have to change anything to be that way. It met our basic needs, and we were there together. It reminded me how much I enjoy and long for simplicity, and it fulfilled that longing. And when we came home to a dishwasher, I had renewed gratitude. But I also brought that simplicity home and leaned more into getting rid of excess as well as just letting things be instead of looking as often at how to change or "improve" them.

With this simple cabin story, I could have internalized a different message altogether. Instead of soaking up the simplicity, the focus could have been on the imperfections or what it was lacking.

So what are the messages we're taking away from our own home? With some time and mental work, I've been able to shift the undercurrent I feel in my own home from "I'm not good enough" to "Only God is perfect, and He made me in His image." My perspective has also shifted from "it's not done" to "it serves us," and from "there's lots of work to do" to "I choose this and will work on our home on my terms and my time." When we do this work of choosing empowering thoughts, the fruits of the labor will go beyond these four walls into our hearts, relationships, and our contributions to the world. We will show up better. And that, my friends, is the good life.

Exercise

What are some thoughts you have in your own home right now? (These may be unintentional like "I'm a slob," "I'm not good enough," "This isn't finished," "This is beautiful," "This is cluttered," etc. Feel free to just write whatever flows out, good or bad, and then we'll work on changing them to intentional thoughts if they aren't serving you) _______________________

____

____

____

Do you like the thoughts you have now? ___________________________

If there are any thoughts that aren't serving you, take one thought at a time and sit with what it could become. (Example: "I'm a slob" may become "I give myself rest" or "it's okay to lower the standard for this season" if you have young kids, are struggling with a health issue, or are just starting this work for

---

example. "There's so much to do" may become "God gives me enough time for everything that needs to get done." "This house is too small" may become "I'm grateful that God gives us what we need" or "This is too cluttered" may be replaced with "I'm learning to let go of what doesn't serve me")

Old Thought: ____

Replacement: ____

Old Thought: ____

Replacement: ____

Old Thought: ____

Replacement: ____

This may be specific to each room, too. Walking in the kitchen may bring up different thoughts than the bedroom. If there's one space that seems to be a trigger, try to discover what thought is creating that effect and come up with a replacement.

This is relevant to making a house a home because these unseen thoughts and habits build the foundation for what is seen. In Stephen Covey's timeless bestseller *The 7 Habits of Highly Effective People*, he explains how the first three habits he teaches are the "Private Victories" that happen within us. Like the foundation of a house, these lay the groundwork for the "Public Victories" that come later. In the same way, the internal work you're doing now in these pages creates the foundation for your home to be not only beautiful and personal but also a fulfilling place for you to thrive.

One great epiphany that came along the way is the realization of just how many people I have met who don't feel comfortable inviting someone into their home. This could be someone who has just moved in, someone who has lived in their home for decades, and everything in between. If this is you in any way, please know you are not alone. I have seen this often, and I think that because there are those people mixed in who are comfortable enough in their own space to open the door, we forget just how many are feeling too ashamed to share the space we spend so much time in...

If we don't feel comfortable allowing someone else to see our space, how can we possibly feel comfortable in our own skin at the place we call "home?" There are solutions; you can feel at home, and you are doing the work right now to get there.

Standing in direct contrast to this is the example of Ron and Jane's vacation rental. They had rented a house for the week in the summer. It was an older home near a lake. At the time, they had three teenagers, and they invited so many people in that the luggage lined the edges of the living room! Teenagers' backpacks and sleeping bags were everywhere. There was also lots of food out to feed those incessantly hungry, growing kids. But none of that took away from this homey place because Ron and Jane didn't care. They didn't let it bother them, so it didn't bother any of us. Jane did the dishes, so it was kept up, but then she relaxed instead of trying to uncover all the kitchen countertops from the bags of chips, so we as their guests all relaxed too. There wasn't even a chair for each person who was there, yet they shared their vacation rental with all of us, and we were all blessed by it as we played games into the night. What a testament to how we can live and be in our homes, no matter how temporary or permanent.

A solution to this is to ask what to let go of and what to cling to. What matters most to you in your home? What is the number one aspect of the home that makes it feel uncomfortable for you, or if it's easier to ask it a different way, what makes it uncomfortable for you to invite someone in? Is this true? Is this shame false or a fear that can be conquered, or is this God gently showing you a habit or other subtle change you can make?

Before I had a husband and family, in some ways it was simpler since I could just pick what I liked, keep the space open, and not have to blend it with anyone else. Friends would walk in and say, "Oh, this is so Maya." While I hadn't yet learned to really settle in, unwind and recharge at home, I liked that they could see my personality and values in the home I'd created. Now that it's Dave and me with our children, even though there are more considerations, in some ways it's simpler than ever. Like how a caterpillar becomes a butterfly, it won't ever be the little Maya house again, but now home is wherever that man is with me and these bouncy kiddos are with us. I said it when I married him and will say it now: I'll follow him anywhere. Because Dave is home.

That takes some pressure off, doesn't it? Does the design, the lighting, the layout make a difference? Of course, those elements both deserve our attention and make it worth our while when we give it to them. But at the end of the day, they're just not the most important part of home. They can change the feel of a room for the better, so a little understanding in this area can go a long way. That's why a whole chapter of this book is dedicated to understanding some of those elements. But there's a reason for the saying "Home is where the heart is." Because something much deeper and more meaningful is at play that cannot be replaced with good design.

Feeling of Home

How do you want to feel in your home? For me, I want to feel like I can kick off my shoes and my expectations. Like I can just be me, be vulnerable, be accepted, laugh, rest, recover, recharge, and then be ready to go back out into the world to do the work that God created me to do.

I want to feel like I get to tidy it up when I want, on my terms, so if it gets a little messy as we live our lives, that's okay with me. I trust myself to put it back in order. Most of the time, I like to clean up the kitchen right after making muffins, but I'm in charge, not the dishes.

Exercise

Those ideas may work for you, but you get to choose in your home. What thoughts do you choose?

____

____

____

____

Stepping Back

A home has four walls, but what matters most can't even be seen. It's love. It's acceptance. It's the hearts, minds, and souls inside, how they treat each other, and how they make each other feel. It starts with how we treat ourselves, how we accept ourselves, and how we love ourselves. No matter what others say or believe about us, if we are inside our own minds telling ourselves that we're failures or will never amount to anything, or whatever other unkind self-talk we may engage in, will we ever feel at home?

This mental work is unseen but powerful. It may be more difficult than painting a wall or putting up pretty artwork. It requires us to have conversations with ourselves, with the immature, primitive parts of our brains that can be both harsh and overdramatic in an effort to keep us safe. A powerful thing happens when we can separate ourselves from that archaic part of our brains that cares about nothing but finding berries and staying in the cave to protect us from saber-toothed tigers. The good news? As we learn to be more comfortable in our own skin, we can learn to feel incredibly comfortable in our own homes.

Key Takeaways:

- Home is first about the intangible feelings of love, welcome, connection, and comfort more than material possessions. When it's rightly ordered, physical changes can help set the ambiance to find those feelings even easier.

- Authenticity and empowering thoughts help create a peaceful and positive home environment, first within ourselves, and then between our walls.

- When we're ready, and if it suits you, hospitality is a beautiful practice and spiritual gift focused on serving and connecting with loved ones and guests.

Chapter 2

Clearing the Ground

Home is far simpler than we sometimes realize, and that also makes it far more attainable. By bringing our ideas to the surface and questioning them, we can find freedom from some of the false notions and expectations we may be creating for ourselves. Some of these may not be a hangup for you, so feel free to flip through these and read the ones that you need to uproot. Let's start clearing the grounds by debunking some of the home myths. Then we'll uproot fears that need to go. Once that space is opened up, we can put in some life-giving permissions and perspective to fill our homes and hearts with the truth.

Myth #1: Home Takes Years to Achieve.

We don't have to spend 20 years homesteading before it can feel like home. For a couple of years, my husband and I focused on remodeling and improving. We were never content with where we were. Our son Cole sensed our restlessness, and one day, after two years in our home, he said, "I feel more at home in a hotel than here." Unfortunately, back then, we hadn't yet learned how to be content with where we were while still working toward what could be. It had nothing to do with how long we had lived in our home or how long we were staying in the hotel room. But it had everything to do with the fact that we were satisfied and content in that hotel room, which we weren't trying to renovate! Now we've brought that contentment home.

Myth #2: Building a Home Requires Novelty

We put in a rock-climbing wall, a chalkboard wall, and monkey bars in our 8-year-old son Cole's room. We also have a ping pong table in the basement and a basketball hoop in the front driveway. Yet Cole, even after all those fun, novel, and exciting additions, asked for home. He wanted to go back to the smaller, simpler home we rented on an Air Force base where he lived until he was 6, which didn't offer any of those perks. We couldn't change the contractor-grade light fixtures or choose the carpet, but it was simple. One of his favorite activities was to go out back and dig in the dirt just beyond the backyard. When friends came over, the kids all gravitated to that simple dirt patch.

All of us missed that home at different times and in different ways before we learned how to recreate home here. Home is simpler than we sometimes make it. Eventually, Dave and I realized that as long as we were feeling unsatisfied, as long as we believed that this house needed to be changed or improved to be home, the kids would feed off that energy. When we finally got off the hamster wheel of making the next improvement or adding that new, novel aspect and allowed ourselves and our home to feel good enough, everyone settled in.

The novelty didn't take away the feeling of home, but the idea that it HAS to be novel did. Once we let go of it, we could have fun adding in novelty when and how we wanted.

Myth #3: Home Has to Be Permanent.

We don't have to wait until we move into our ultimate forever dream home to find home. It's sooner than that. One of those memorable, homey experiences for me was helping a friend move out of her apartment, where we had hung out so many times over the couple of years she lived there. The movers had come, the furniture was all packed, and we sat on the floor where the couch used to be, looking toward the wall where the TV used to rest, listening to music on her phone. It was nostalgic, it was cozy, it brought closure and tied together all those fun, carefree memories in that apartment. That was both the last and the homiest memory in that place, and it happened on the way out the door. If we could feel so at home in the process of moving out of an enjoyable living space, then home can certainly be felt in temporary spaces.

Home for a matter of Hours, Days, Weeks, Years, or just one little lifetime

"Come in. Make yourself at home!" We've probably all heard this phrase from an inviting host as they welcomed us into their home. But how can that be if we're only passing through as a guest? How can we be at home in a temporary space, knowing that we may be leaving in a couple of hours? Yet somehow we do, right? We may kick off our shoes, sit back and relax, grab a drink, and prioritize connecting with someone we value over checking off to-dos. And it does bring a feeling of homeliness.

Right now, as I'm writing this, I've made myself at home in a cozy, Victorian, historic bed and breakfast, with a very hospitable owner/operator named Rachel. My temporary desk is a textured pillow across my lap with the laptop computer sitting on top, and my legs are up as I sit sideways across a vintage loveseat. The baby is napping in the pack 'n play while the older two kids enjoy a little quiet with the toys they proudly packed themselves in their backpacks. Dave is catching a little nap to make up for the disrupted sleep last night in a new setting. We brought the comfort of the familiar routines with us, and everyone seems to be feeling pretty settled. Have you ever felt at home on a vacation, as a guest in someone else's home, or in another temporary space that you were passing through? What made it feel that way to you?

One reason it felt homey to me is that I was living in the present moment, not thinking about what I plan to do later or what's on a to-do list somewhere. Sometimes in a fresh space, it's easier for me to put those burdens down and just be.

Another homey aspect for me is that the owner was so hospitable and welcoming. She has the gift of service and hospitality. She made us feel so welcome and at home, and we accepted that hospitality.

These examples serve as evidence that we can be at home before we have our "perfect" forever home. This is to debunk the idea that we have to wait that long. Even in the dream home, when we move into it, we think we'll feel settled once it's all decorated and organized. So we do all those things, but then the kids grow and hobbies change, and we think it'll happen once it's changed to fit this new season of life. Then the styles change, so we think once we get new furniture and decor to update our forever dream home, we'll be ready. Then we think when we remodel, or get nicer grown-up furniture, or add the deck, etcetera, etcetera, etcetera. Doesn't it feel stressful even just to read those words? It felt stressful to write them. Surely that's not the way to feel at home, so let's take a deeper dive here at this idea, so we can uproot the fallacy that may be keeping us from enjoying our home now, no matter how temporary...

Exercise

Think of a time when you felt at home in a place that you knew you wouldn't be staying in. Do you have that space and feeling in your mind? The balcony on a vacation, a visit with a loved one, a camping trip, wherever it was for you. Describe: _______________________________

____

____

What was it that made it feel so homey? Was it the scenery? Was it being in the moment? Was it rest? Was it excitement and adventure? Was it connection? Was it a combination of items? _______________________

____

Now that you've remembered a time you felt at home in a temporary space and identified what made it feel that way, what can you bring into your own space to encapsulate that same homeyness? _______________

____

Hint: It may be a thought, or it may be an object, like a comfy chair to curl up in.

Myth #4: It Has to Be the Perfect Dream Home for it to be Called Home.

I've known two people who have built their dream homes; we're talking serious dream homes—only to later move out. One of those was a multi-million-dollar, absolutely custom-built, oceanfront home in Seattle. He had extensive building experience, and every contractor who worked on it had at least 20 years of experience. No detail was overlooked. For example, the bathroom drawer where the hair dryer would be stored had an outlet inside the drawer so the hair dryer didn't even have to be plugged in and unplugged! Then their family grew, and they moved. Home moved with them, even though the next house wasn't that way, because they were together and were there for good reasons.

The other absolute dream home I visited was on the island of Kauai, overlooking the ocean. It was so beautiful, so original, and absolutely stunning. Then they got a job opportunity in Costa Rica, and they moved out. They made their home in another country.

These stories show that home moves with us, not with our possessions. It's wonderful to dream, and the journey along the way is where the juice of life comes in. Sometimes, in dreaming about our home, we come up with changes that have a big impact and that we can use in our space where we are now. What you long for in your home is worth the pursuit. Also, now is a good time to enjoy today. Life changes, and wherever we are right now can be home if there's love inside. "Love your neighbor as yourself."

Myth #5: Home Has to be Expensive

Home doesn't have to be the most expensive, and in fact, often the costliest option isn't the homiest. It also doesn't have to be the ultimate thrifting game. Spending money on quality pieces that bring you joy can be wonderful. Even more important than the price point is being true to ourselves. There's something powerful about the simple question, "what do I want?" or "what do I like?" It helps us step back from the trendy or from what we've been told we're supposed to like and want. There's a beautiful relief that comes from asking that question and giving ourselves an honest answer. We may like staying relevant to the trends and having expensive quality pieces, but it's our choice.

Myth #6: Home Has to be Perfect.

Sometimes the imperfections in our home give us permission to show up with our own imperfections, if we have the right attitude about them. The imperfections can also make us feel like we're screwing up, but the beauty is we get to decide what we think of it.

When Dave was coming home from a trip, I used to get anxious about getting the house all picked up, clean, and ready for him. The intention was good since he likes a clean and tidy home, but the outcome was that he would return to a clean house and a frazzled wife! Because I was stressing about having our house perfect, he would do the same. Instead of getting a break when he got home, he would immediately find something that hadn't been cleaned or taken care of yet and get to work. He wanted to ease my burden so I wouldn't be stressed. What a spiral!

I still make an effort to take care of our home and tidy up for Dave. The change is that it's not frantic anymore. Real people live here, so messes get made and then cleaned up. I want him to come home to peace, not perfection. One day in particular, I was really at ease when he got home. Instead of immediately finding the next task to do to help me around the house, Dave sat down on the couch with me and relaxed. Perfect housekeeping doesn't hold a candle to the permission to just be.

When we made design changes in our home, it was for a purpose, not perfection. "What does it feel like?" I asked the two beautiful neighbor girls. They had come to our home for the first time since we'd made the changes: the new dining table, the dining bench to load kids on, and comfortable plush dining chairs with the curved, antique-style chandeliers over the table; the spacious, soft rug in the living room with the new oversized mirrors hanging on the wall that invited you to dance or play or get cozy; the antique farm bench in the entryway.

"Organized," said the younger girl with just a little sass, "we could use some of that in our house."

The older sister didn't answer right away. She thought for a minute, smiled, and looked up at me. "It feels like God and Jesus are here next to me, and here on my other side, and all around here in this home."

I was amazed at how that young girl could feel the heart of our home. She could feel the presence of God in this home that is our domestic church. This is why we do this work, so that we can feel the presence of God, His peace and love, in our spaces.

Myth #7: Home Has to be Immaculate.

One of the thoughts I return to often in our home is that real people live here. I don't feel the need to apologize for our home. We generally keep it relatively tidy because that's important to my husband and me, but I don't clean the floors after every meal.

There's also an ebb and flow to this. On days when I may be tired or not feeling well, I give myself permission to relax the standards a bit and walk past certain chores guilt-free. Other times, I may be inspired to take on a mess or organization project that's been tucked away for a bit. Thank goodness home doesn't have to be immaculate every day. Most of us would rarely get to experience it!

Tip: Keep at least one area or countertop clean and tidy. For example, if the kids made a fort or we're in the middle of a project in the living room, then I'd like the dining room table cleared off and the dining area clean. This gives me a place to rest my eyes and a room to retreat to that feels good until the other area is put back together.

Figuring out what is holding you back

We're going to step into the places in our minds that may be messy, because that is how we clean them up. I have found that when my mind is clear, decluttering my home is almost effortless.

One of the beauties of this mind work is that it doesn't cost anything and doesn't rely on a contractor's schedule. We don't have to wait until we've saved up enough and planned a remodel. Start by asking your brain, "Brain, what do you think of me, and why do you think I am not completely happy with this home?" and just listen to the answer that comes from within yourself.

Then remind your brain who you are: a human being with innate dignity and value, made with a purpose, loved unconditionally by your creator, precious and worthy. Positive affirmations are daily work, and most of the time we don't want to do them. It is worth the effort. On the days when I've done the work of encouraging myself, the whole flow improves. On the days when I let my brain stay in self-deprecating places, much is wasted.

For the second part of the question, "Why do you think I am not completely happy with this home?" just let the thoughts flow out. It could be tangible items like a lack of storage (solutions for solving those issues are coming as you keep reading). It could relate to the work of homemaking, which can be helped with systems (also discussed later in this book). The third option is that it can relate to beliefs, fears, and mindset.

Here are some of the fears that can hold us back in our homes.

Fear of not having enough.

Sometimes we cling to what we don't need out of fear that we may need it or may not have what we need. This is big for me as my mom grew up in great scarcity where the skill of stretching and repurposing was far more necessary than it is for most of us today. What's the antidote? Faith. Trusting that it is enough. Faith to let go of excess and to live in a way that makes sense today.

Fear of not being enough.

Have you ever noticed what it feels like when you try too hard to prove that you're enough? Have you also ever had the opposite experience of showing up as you are without trying to prove yourself? The difference is in the driving force. Are you driven by the desire to impress others because, deep down, you actually don't feel like you're good enough? Or does your drive come from a subtle confidence that you're enough and can just be who you are?

On days when I'm feeling good, somehow that great outfit just comes out of my closet. On days when I'm feeling inadequate, nothing looks quite right, and somehow, in the same closet with the same wardrobe, I can't find anything that makes me feel comfortable in my own skin. I think our homes are an extension of that too.

The good news is that confidence can be learned and grows with each experience of it! When we don't feel adequate, we try too hard in our homes. Maybe we make it too fancy, too complicated, or too "impressive," but whatever it is, it's not quite our true selves. But when we're rooted in the truth that you are "fearfully and wonderfully made," then we can feel comfortable in our own skin and in our own home.

I think often the reason we don't feel at home is that, for some reason, we have convinced ourselves that our home isn't 'good enough.' Maybe it's the plans we have that no one knows about, and internally that makes us feel like our home isn't "finished" or good or right. Perhaps it's a comparison to someone else or Pinterest. Maybe it's a mess, it's not as organized as we'd like, family pictures aren't updated; the list goes on and on of what we can make up.

Often, when I go into someone's home, especially if it's a short or unexpected visit, they'll apologize for the condition of the home. My response is, "Hey, I live in the real world! People actually live in our home too." If you've ever felt any of these, recognize that this is a common human feeling. It stems from our own expectations, which we make up and that we can change. Tony Robbins, international inspirational speaker and entrepreneur, says, "Trade your expectations for appreciation."

Exercise

If you relate to these, take a moment now to do this exercise. Seriously this is less than 5 minutes and will help you intentionally choose how you want to feel in your home.

1. How do I feel in my own home, especially when someone comes over?

   ____

   ____

2. Shake it out. Put your hands in the air. Stand up and stretch. Take 3 breaths. Now, how do you want to feel in your space? Think about a time when you felt really good. Why did it feel so good? Was it outside under a tree? Was it a space no one else could come into so there were no expectations on you? Was it cozy or exciting or peaceful? How do you want to feel in your home?

   ____

   ____.

3. What's one change you can make that will move you in that direction? Is it a thought you'll choose like "I'm good enough" or "this is for me?" Is it bringing a bag over and clearing out some items that feel like clutter? Is it bringing in a special, sentimental item and putting it somewhere you'll see it everyday? There's no right or wrong answer because this if for you. _______________

   ____.

4. Do the one thing in #3, or if it's not something that can be done right now, put it on the calendar and commit to it. Action feels good. Intentional action takes us out of a negative state and moves us forward.

5. Celebrate. You did it!

Fear of vulnerability.

Sometimes it's easier to hide behind the latest trends than to be true to who we are because of the fear that others won't like us or what we like. Brené Brown, in her book *Gifts of Imperfection*, says, "Healthy striving is self-focused: 'How can I improve?' Perfectionism is other-focused: 'What will they think?'"

It's so grounding to stop and ask, "What do I like?"

I can feel confused about what I like, and then somehow, when I stop and ask myself the question, I'm surprised at how often I know the answer. It also helps me to stop thinking of guests or people coming into our home for a moment. This is for us first. This is a haven for the people living here. Then, from the extension of that, sure, we may sometimes host people we care about for dinner, coffee, happy hour, or an extended visit, but that's not why I'm creating this. That comes from the overflow. When I'm struggling to be authentic, I like to take that off the table and refocus on just me and just us.

We are told to "love our neighbor as ourselves." When we first love ourselves well, it gives us energy and empowers us to love others. Think about the people you admire, and I wonder if, like it is for me, you'll see that they take care of themselves. We also serve those in our lives better when we take care of ourselves. This looks beautiful on us because it looks right.

So I give you permission to ask, "What do I want? What do I like?"

Authenticity takes a certain amount of vulnerability. When we were choosing light fixtures for our dining room, I started out with a modern, simple set of black, round, hanging fixtures. To me, those were safe since they're trending now, and I do like some modern style. Only by coming to a place of being vulnerable enough to show up as I really am was I able to switch to the beautiful, rustic chandeliers that now hang in our dining room. The reason it relates to vulnerability is that they are what I actually like, so it feels like if people don't like them, they don't like that part of me. But you know what? Who cares? At first, I couldn't say that, but now I can. I like them and have wanted chandeliers for a long time. Doing this work, the work that you are doing right now, is what brought me to a place of authenticity in our home so that our style choices were genuine.

Then the balance to that is that what I want more than to have any dream piece of furniture or decor or image in my mind of my home is to have peace and unity with the people living in this home with me. Remind yourself what is most important to you about your home.

Dave and I had an experience recently in the kitchen where we were planning to put a light cream plaster on the walls to give it an Old European vibe and a finished pop. Halfway through the job, there was a darker concrete color drying on the walls that was simply an underlayment for the cream color. Dave loved the darker look. Since it's rare for him to have a strong reaction like that, I knew I had to honor it. I wanted to honor it. But the win for me was not just accepting the color that was there, even though he would have been happy with it, because I didn't quite like it.

What I realized later is that if I had settled for that darker color that he liked and ignored my own desires, every time I walked into our kitchen, it would have rubbed me just a little wrong. Since it was a decision for my husband, it would have made me feel things like "I don't get what I want because of him" or "I'm settling for what Dave likes" or "we have to choose between him being happy and me being happy." You get the idea. It took courage and, I think, love for myself, worthiness, as well as a little work, to find a darker color that I did like too. The end result was not just something I liked even more than the original cream, but something Dave liked even better than his original dark color choice. That never would have happened if I hadn't loved myself too.

Now when I see it, the subtle messages are things like "Dave and I are a good team" and "what we create together is better than what either of us would do on our own." What a huge difference. Rather than subtly tugging against us, it brings us together. It honors both of us individually and together. And the path to get there was me having the courage to stand up for myself. Perhaps this is why God has told us to love others "as ourselves."

Honoring what we each like

Permissions and Perspective

Giving ourselves permission can create a powerful psychological shift by releasing internal resistance and shifting us to a place of authenticity and confidence. When we give ourselves permission, it has been found to reduce inner conflict, affirm self-worth, release the need for external approval, encourage action, and open up space for experimentation, play, and creativity. Fun! As it relates to our homes, this helps us accept our homes the way they are, stop chasing perfection, and feel empowered to playfully create a space we love.

There are times in my life when I simply need permission, and I have learned that often, that can come from me. This isn't me giving you permission but rather inviting you to give yourself permission in any of the following areas you may need or want. This list of permissions can also help you brainstorm any other permissions you may be ready to give yourself.

We live in a productive world where rest is often thought of as an unnecessary luxury, or perhaps even as the nemesis of hard work. Please don't take this as me suggesting we sit on the couch all day. I do suggest that when we really give ourselves permission to take a load off, to fully unwind, to plug into our power source of God Himself and feel true joy and peace, we will in fact be more productive when it's time. We will connect better with our loved ones. We will be more likely to love ourselves and others and to create a home that does the same. We will live more fully.

Worthy Because God Makes us Worthy

God chooses to live in imperfect homes. He tells us in 1 Corinthians 6:19, "Do you not know that your bodies are temples of the Holy Spirit, who is in you, whom you have received from God?" He makes His home inside us. The first home we build and nurture is within ourselves. At the same time, there's a moment in Scripture when a Roman centurion—an outsider with no religious credentials—looks at Jesus and says, "Lord, I am not worthy that you should enter under my roof, but only say the word..." Through these two verses, we learn:

1. **We are not worthy on our own.** That may sound harsh, but it's actually freeing. We all have feelings of inadequacy and unworthiness. Good news! That makes us normal and sane. That makes us in alignment with truth because we are all imperfect. Fortunately, that's not the end of our story. The Centurion received the healing he humbly asked for, even in his unworthiness, and God does the same for you and for me. The truth is, we don't have to be

worthy when we serve a God who fills in the cracks, as long as we're showing up and doing the best we can, which is probably better some days than others. He knows exactly what we are like, exactly where we struggle, exactly where we feel the most inadequate. And he chooses to make His home inside us anyway. He chooses to love us exactly as we are. Even better, he designed us for a specific purpose, like a carpenter builds a chair for a purpose and does not see the chair as falling short for not making an effective table.

2. **He makes us whole.** Jesus doesn't leave us there wallowing in our own 'unworthiness.' He brings us the answer on how to be healed, how to be made whole, how to enter into our fullest and greatest potential. He holds the key, and He IS the key to unlocking the greatest mysteries of our homes and souls. He cleans out the greatest depths of our beings. He enters into our messiest spaces with us, gets down on His glorious 'hands and knees' and does the dirtiest work with us. There is no distance too far for Him to travel with us. He is the ultimate lover and our greatest romance.

When we do the work between our ears, in our hearts, and in our souls to love who we are, to feel worthy of the blessings that have come into our lives because of Him, and to walk in that truth, the rewards are abundant. It's interesting how, when we make a decision from a place of feeling unworthy, it's not generally a good decision. We don't buy the thing we really want for our home but still spend the money on something we don't like as much (because we can wrap our minds around the idea of being worthy of it). You. Are. Worthy.

Proverbs 13:12: "Hope deferred makes the heart sick, but a longing fulfilled is a tree of life."

God wants to fulfill the deepest desires of our hearts. Ultimately, the very deepest desire is for love, which is God. To feel at home is also a holy desire.

To bring beauty into the world in the piece of Earth that God has entrusted to us is good work. And when this longing within us is fulfilled, it is a tree of life.

This is the breakthrough that happened for me. I had said, "I really want to see this all the way through, and I might need help to make that happen." The decor, the finishing touches, the real plants—those items with a small price tag that are easy to put up for some reason stopped me in my tracks. Those may not be an issue for you, but I would make excuses each time we'd find one about why it just wasn't quite right. After months, a pattern emerged, and we had stagnated. So I leaned in to break through, and this is what I realized...

Let Yourself Buy <u>the</u> Thing

Have you ever had that thing, and I bet you have, that may or may not be expensive, but for some reason, your mind tells you that YOU can't have THAT thing, even though you really want it? Maybe as I'm saying this, there's an item coming to your mind, and you can feel your body changing – maybe your breath is picking up, your heartbeat is just a little faster, and you're having to be intentional to breathe. Can you identify that thing? If not, that's okay too. Can you relate to that feeling?

The funny thing is, somewhere in our minds, we seem to decide that for some reason we can't have that thing we really want. And so, we buffer, and we go spend the same resources, if not more, on something else that we're able to believe we can have but isn't even really what we want. We spend the same amount of money that one item would have cost on something else that isn't fulfilling. We spend the time that we had available to go get that by picking up a cup of coffee or something else. We're left longing.

The truth is, there's not an endless number of items that we actually want. If we really think about it, there's probably some reason, although not a true one, that we're using as a reason to convince ourselves that we can't have that thing. For me, having an upgraded shower head was that item. I would pass by them in the store and gaze longingly at them, but then my mind would tell me I couldn't have it, and I would move on. This happened for years! Every shower would be a subtle reminder of how nice it would be to upgrade the stream of water, but somewhere in my mind was the nagging thought that I couldn't do that. We had the money, but it wasn't that; it was some limiting belief in my mind. I think the item itself is something different for each of us.

If you can relate to this, and especially if there's something that has come to your mind as you're reading this, let this serve as permission to get it. You're worth it. The only caveat is that if you haven't saved up the money yet, you can choose to wait until then.

How do you identify when this is happening? Let me encourage you first that it gets easier with time and practice. We start to notice the pattern and familiar emotions that come up when this is something we really want but haven't yet given ourselves permission to get.

A HUGE hack that has helped me with this is giving. Let me explain. At the root of feeling unworthy of what I truly desire is this awareness all of us have of the inequalities in the world. Here's this opportunity for me to get something I really want, especially if it's more of a luxury than a necessity, and yet I know there are billions of people in the world whose basic needs aren't being met. Then I feel guilty (why do I get to live such a good life?) and talk myself out of it. The problem? Now I'm unfulfilled, and the basic needs of all those people still are not met! The solution? Give ourselves permission to live the best life we can and feel grateful. Trade guilt for gratitude. ALSO, from that place of gratitude, give in some way to those in need. Don't forget the poor. This feels _so_ good. If you don't believe me, I challenge you to try it, even just with a $5 item to start where you give $5 too. Currently, giving

$5 to Feeding America, for example, provides at least 50 meals here in our country to the hungry. Now, every time you see that thing you really wanted and let yourself get it, you not only get the joy of the item itself, you also get the joy of the story and the impact your life had because you were willing to give to yourself and others.

Have you ever tried to be generous with someone who is generous? It seems like no matter what I would do for them, their kind heart would pour back into me what felt like more than I gave to them. God is the ultimate giver. He won't be outdone in His generosity. Matthew 7:11 says, "If you, then, though you are evil, know how to give good gifts to your children, how much more will your Father in heaven give good gifts to those who ask him!"

The year we remodeled our kitchen, we gave the most we ever had. I don't share this to brag; in fact, I would prefer not to share it, but I include it here to show how God worked through us accepting good gifts from Him. I was overwhelmed by the generosity of God in my life that I could have such a wonderful space, and from the overflow of my heart came a generosity that I had not been able to experience up to that point. This is one way of loving others as ourselves. This is God's word in action, and it can happen within our homes and through our homes.

From Scarcity to Abundance

Sometimes we avoid spending even a little on our homes if we can't afford a complete overhaul, leading to a sense of lack in our daily lives. We might also hold onto items we don't like simply because we have them. This scarcity mindset doesn't serve us.

One manifestation of this occurred with our dining room table. I grew up with a simple, homemade picnic-style table. Later, I had a free, basic oval table. When Dave and I married, our table was a small, somewhat unattractive hand-me-down that Dave refinished. Despite a major home remodel, we kept this old, small table for years, even as our family grew.

Shifting Perspective

Recently, I found a beautiful, discounted dining set that surprisingly appealed to me, even with features I had previously disliked. This felt like a breakthrough. Although we didn't buy it due to a mismatch in person, my perspective shifted. I realized we would eventually get the right table.

This experience also gave me a new appreciation for our existing table. Instead of seeing its flaws, I now cherish the memories created around it: a toddler's exploration, early family holidays, and countless everyday moments. Its imperfections tell a story of our life together.

Embracing Both/And

Now, I can simultaneously appreciate our current table for its sentimental value and look forward to a future one that better suits our needs. It's no longer an either/or situation, but a both/and. Our humble table reminds me to be present and value today, even while anticipating future joys.

This personal journey with a simple wood table revealed deeper truths about my own limiting beliefs and the power of shifting perspective. Identifying these disconnects can unlock what holds us back from fully embracing our lives and homes.

Permission to Let It Take Time

Johanna Gaines, designer and TV star from the show Fixer Upper, left her living room wall bare until the right item came along. Then one day, she found a giant clock with the hands broken off. For her, that symbolized this idea of carefree timelessness in the living room, and she decided it was the perfect piece to finish off the space. It's okay to wait and let some parts of our home take time.

Permission for It to Be Fast

If your home comes together effortlessly and quickly, that's great too! Go for it. Often, our best decisions are made quickly and from the gut.

Permission to Give Yourself Grace

I have learned to give myself permission to not force it. Sometimes the right idea hasn't come yet. Sometimes it's not the time to put resources into it yet. That's okay. If either of those is true for your situation, then it gives you permission to have peace as it is now, and that feels like home.

Since we have a staircase that goes about five steps down into the yard, we had envisioned adding a covered deck on the back of the house. We thought we'd figured it out. This would give us a place to sit and eat meals that would be protected from the elements, so we could use the back more often. We were planning to add grapevines on the west side of the deck to keep the evening sun from blasting us from the side. It sounded like an upgrade, and we knew it would come at a hefty price tag, but this is home, right? Fortunately, before we pulled the trigger on the add-on, I casually asked a landscape designer what she thought of the idea. We had told her our plans, but when we saw her again, I simply asked her what she would do if she had a blank slate. Thank God I did. That five-minute conversation changed our minds.

She said, "I wouldn't do it. Right now, when you walk outside, it feels like a sanctuary, like the outdoors. If you added the deck, it would feel more like an extension of the indoors, and you would lose that lovely outdoor feeling you get when you walk out back"— my favorite part of the home.

Then she went on to suggest making a back patio area out of brick pavers and simply pouring polymeric sand in between the pavers. She said it seems counterintuitive to just hold the pavers together with sand, but that it makes them age well. Over time, especially with the trees nearby, the pavers get a natural wave to them, and it only adds to the charm. Then, if we ever wanted to level the pavers back out, we simply pull up the ones that have gotten too high, remove some of the sand under them, and place them back in. The same roots that give those pavers the waves that add character and charm would cause cracks in concrete or in pavers cemented together.

She said we can even add a retaining wall around the pavers to distinguish the area as well as create extra seating. Doesn't it sound lovely? Once we heard her suggestions, the idea of the deck we had been prepared to invest so much into creating lost its appeal. That investment of $250 for her landscape design work ended up saving us thousands of dollars and helping us get to a home we enjoy more.

Permission to Make Changes and Change Our Minds

Be willing to put a nail hole in the wall and then take whatever hung there down and move it later. Try it, and if you don't like it, change your mind. Better yet, change it around just for fun and to keep it fresh.

Rob and Amy know something about making a house a home. Wherever she lives, it's a pleasant place to be. Each home has offered its advantages and its weak points, but each has been beautiful, functional, and warm and welcoming, with pleasant scents in the air and a well-placed speaker for background music. Each has been given time and thought to make the space work for them, their family, and their guests. Each has been filled with their inviting hospitality, laughter, and generosity.

On one visit, they had just hung a new set of light fixtures over the kitchen island. It was a central location in the home and one of the first areas you saw upon entering, so it was a small item that packed a big punch. We complimented the glass light fixtures, and Amy simply said, "We don't like them." It wasn't in a spoiled or obnoxious way, just a simple matter-of-fact statement. They tried them, and they didn't end up liking them. They shared that this was the second set of light fixtures they had bought and installed there since they didn't end up liking the first ones either. Spoiler alert: in the end, the third set of lights ended up being the ones they liked.

That simple statement blew my mind. It had never occurred to me that it might be okay to buy a fixture, install it, not like it, buy another one, and change it. I would not have given myself permission in the past to make that choice. If I didn't like it, I would have lived with it forever. That puts some high stakes for me on making the right decision the first time, and I don't always make the right decision! Who does? It's so liberating to be able to change our minds and for that to be totally okay.

The third set of light fixtures that Rob and Amy installed really was a better choice. They fit the home better. They were interesting without demanding to be the center of attention. They were right; it was worth the effort.

Rest and Relaxation: Permission to Just "Be" at Home

One homey story I've heard more than once from my mom is when she went to my grandparents' home for the first time. She and my dad were dating, and she was nervous to meet my dad's parents. Ignoring social etiquette, the first thing my grandma Mary did was invite my mom into the kitchen with her to help with the dishes. It was a weight off my mom's shoulders and made her feel right at home from the start.

Our longtime friend Aaron Bourbon opened the door to let us in and then walked right back to his living room, where he plopped down comfortably on the couch. He was comfortable in his own skin and in his own space. There was confidence. And since he was relaxed, it was an invitation for us to kick back too. He didn't mix us drinks or impress us. He just was. We felt right at home.

Perhaps because of these influences to model, I experienced this when my friend Rob came to visit, and I made the conscious decision to prioritize time and conversation with my friend over serving him. We ended up laughing about the hodgepodge of treats I pulled out of the fridge. At one point, there was just a bowl of baby carrots on the table and a couple of lattes! But we connected and had such a wonderful, carefree visit. In a way, this was me choosing my friend over my own ego of being a "great hostess." It was delightful.

These stories are beautiful because they remind us to keep it simple. They give us permission to relax and just be.

Permission for Seasons of Life to Be Different

"I'm looking forward to having a beautiful home one day," my friend Lilly told her husband. "You will," he replied, "but right now we're taking care of my sick mom." Lilly made the conscious, intentional decision to use her time and resources for the care of a loved one who was battling cancer. Isn't that a homey and loving decision for her to make in that circumstance?

She still takes care of her home, keeping it safe and making sure it works for her and her family, but this wasn't the season for going all in on gorgeous stuff. Not yet. Isn't that a home filled with love, welcome, unity, and intentionality? For you, God could be inviting you to have the gorgeous home of your dreams, even in a circumstance that doesn't look like it would allow it. This is permission for that too. I'm not here to put limits on you or God.

What makes this idea complete is the next permission...

Permission to Be Led

"This is what I want. It's so inspiring," Katherine said as she walked into our simple, open living room. "We're in a temporary home right now, so we have boxes and haven't really settled in," she continued. I invited her to see how her temporary space could feel like home and kindly challenged her to settle in, giving her tips on storage units and solutions that would work for her home now.

Every time I made a suggestion, she peacefully explained why their home was exactly what they needed and was serving their family well.

"Our kids have never been happier," was one comment. They were in the process of blending their families, and she was approaching it with the feminine grace of honoring the new father of her children, who was leading their family frugally and didn't want a storage unit. Katherine is a go-getter and knows how to create a well-designed house. She knows how to entertain and does it often. Yet in this season, God was leading her to focus on holding the hearts of her children instead of entertaining as much. God was guiding her to uphold a family dynamic of respecting the man whom God had brought her to protect and provide for them. He was also calling all of them to patience as they searched for the home they would be settling into soon.

The only change that happened that day for Katherine was realizing that there was nothing wrong with her home, that it was exactly what God was leading her to embrace right now, and that she could wholeheartedly accept that truth instead of thinking it was supposed to be something else. In these seasons, we can wait in joyful hope. We can also fully embrace the joy and beauty of this moment.

On the other end of the spectrum, sometimes there are seasons when the blessings are so abundant they can be hard to accept. A divinely inspired phrase that covers both truths is, "Do not marvel. Neither should you doubt." When God brings greater abundance than we could imagine, there's no need to marvel. That is the big God that we serve. When we are waiting and wondering when our turn will come, there is no need to doubt. He is the same God then. At the heart of it, the circumstances matter less than being led and letting it be, accepting whatever He gives or takes away on His timing. We can trust in His goodness all the time and simply walk.

Perspective

Perspective is huge because it can completely change the way we look at a room, our home, our lives, and ourselves. And what's equally incredible about perspective is that we can consciously choose it. Like a pair of glasses, perspective is the lens through which we see, and, like glasses, we can take them off or change them if they're making the images look bad.

At one point, after feeling good in our home for some time, I experienced a negative perspective shift. Somehow, I found a way to make everything that I looked at in our home send the message that I had made a mistake and that I was inadequate. The feeling that kept coming up was regret. For example, I would walk into our beautiful front room and think, "Why didn't I think through this room better? What are we going to do in this room? Why did I mess this all up?" Even just looking at the room made me feel bad about myself. What's worse, while I was stuck in this mindset, I was transferring that same idea to several other areas of our home. In the front yard, I would see the new tree that we put in and think, "Why did we do that?" In the living room, I would see our couch and think of something similar that made me feel like I screwed it all up and filled me with regret. In our bedroom, all I could see were the plans that we were considering doing and hadn't pulled the trigger on yet, and I kept thinking again that I was messing everything up.

The thought that finally pulled it all together was when I realized that this perspective made me feel like I wasn't safe in my own home. I didn't feel safe to be who I was. I didn't feel like I was good enough in my own home, in my own skin. I had been wondering why, for the last few days, my stress levels were so high.

With a journal and a pencil in my hand, when I wrote that statement that I didn't feel safe in my own home, I immediately understood why I had felt so stressed. This perspective was robbing me of my peace and turning my home back into a house for some reason. Writing that down and seeing it on paper led to a big sigh of relief. It all made sense.

Once it made sense to me, it all changed. The beautiful front room no longer sent me the message that I did something wrong; it simply meant that we had created a beautiful space. Suddenly, when I looked at that room, instead of feeling inadequate, I felt proud. My bedroom had previously felt incomplete. All of a sudden, it was satisfying. It met all of our needs. The couch that had stirred up so many negative emotions I could see now was really rooted in one feeling: I didn't feel worthy of something nice. But again, once I understood the root of it, instead of dissecting the fabric we chose, I could just be grateful.

Realizing these perspectives that were flowing through my mind as I wandered through my home changed how I felt in four different parts of our home in less than an hour of journaling. Total cost? Zero dollars.

Part of the reason I had been able to get into such a poor perspective was because of this underlying belief that I could make a mistake in our home. I have good news for you: There is no home police! Sure, there are some little simple, easy-to-learn design tips that can serve us by giving us hacks, almost like a cheat code. Those are in the Design Simplified chapter of this book.. But what's even more powerful than that is the gut feeling inside of you that tells you what you like, and I promise you have it.

Tip: There's a difference between thinking about our home in a positive way—"noodling" over fun ideas and dreaming of possibilities—versus "chewing" on our home in a negative way, spiraling, questioning, and doubting. One feels light and playful, while the other feels draining and tiring. Which do you choose? Pay attention to the way it feels when you're thinking about your home. If it feels like chewing, you get to decide if you want to change it.

Key Takeaways

- Home is attainable in temporary spaces and moments; it doesn't need to be a "forever dream home" or take years to create.

- Addressing underlying fears and limiting beliefs about oneself is key to feeling at home and shifting from scarcity to abundance.

- Perspective significantly impacts how one feels about their home, and it can be consciously chosen to prioritize grace, patience, and divine inspiration.

Chapter 3

The Space that Serves You

What if your home doesn't have to impress anyone but you?

That simple question has the power to quiet a thousand scrolling comparisons. In a world saturated with picture-perfect living rooms and curated kitchens, it's easy to forget the most important truth: your home should serve you—your real life, your real needs, and your real rhythm.

We'll look at how to make choices not out of obligation or comparison, but out of clarity and care. We'll also talk about the balance between upkeep and ease—so your home can be both a place that nurtures you and one you're free to enjoy, even before the laundry is folded and the floors are swept.

Is my Home Serving Me, or am I Serving My Home?

Much of what we do and experience in life, and perhaps all of what we do, can be done feeling stressed and overwhelmed, or it can be done as we "laugh at the days to come," as it says in Proverbs 31. The difference is what happens between our ears and in our hearts and souls.

One home we toured had breathtaking views and showcased the work the homeowners had put into it. It was for sale by the owner, and the wife was present when we toured it. At one point, we sat on the back patio soaking in the sweeping view. I asked the homeowner if she enjoyed it, and she replied with something along the lines of, "Well, there's always one more project to do. It's been a lot of work." Right in her backyard was a dream view, and yet she couldn't take a break from serving her house to let her home serve her. There have been days and times when I was just like this woman, too busy running around serving my home to let it serve me.

Of course, having a home, even if that home is a rented room, comes with maintenance and cleaning. We put effort into our home, and then we reap the benefits of it. But that mental shift of realizing that the home is for us and not the other way around can go further in making a house a home than any type of tile or paint color. If you're anything like me, this isn't a one-time thought and then we're done. It's a mentality that improves with practice, and it's worth the effort. It'll create "home" faster than almost anything else we can do.

The Dishes are Not in Charge

For me, the dishes were the spot where I would get sucked into serving our home instead of being served. For some reason, I just generally wouldn't give myself permission to let it go. It was an unnecessary non-negotiable in my mind to get the dishes done before going to bed, which meant sometimes I got to bed really late.

Now, something in me has shifted. We have a deep sink, so I can put dishes down into it without having to look at them if I don't want to get to them right away. I can soak them in water so the job doesn't become twice as tedious. Then, when I'm ready, and when it's on my timeline, I take care of it. The dishes still get done because I value having a clean home for myself and my family. But now I'm in charge, not the silverware. Now it happens when I say so. That might be the next morning or a couple of meals later, or it might be right away, which is still my favorite when it works.

What changed was me giving myself permission to let it go. Sometimes the chores should take a back seat, at least for a little while, so you can have time to rest and take care of yourself and your family. I had a conversation with myself and said I'm enough and our home is enough, even with a few bowls in the sink.

Perhaps dishes aren't the place where this comes up for you, but is there some part of the home that you feel like you constantly have to serve? Is it laundry, tidying up, floors, countertops, or something else? My invitation to you is to first check in with yourself and ask why. Perhaps it's simply a mental shift.

We Can Do Things We Don't Want to Do

On the other hand, sometimes we may struggle to stop putting our feet up long enough to do the chores! The challenge may be getting ourselves to do those mundane tasks that are rarely gratifying at the moment. We may get so used to seeing the messes and apologizing for them that we forget how effective a little power clean can be and how good it feels afterward.

Tip: Most simple chores take less time than we think. If keeping up with housework is a struggle, try fitting in just a quick extra chore or two in the little gaps of your day. Then be proud of yourself when you get it done!

We may simply lack good systems and benefit from learning a few tools. That's why we have a chapter dedicated to home routines, including tips for power cleaning and easy ways to figure out how long your ordinary tasks take so you can fit them in the right spots in your day. We'll also discuss practical solutions to 'catch-all' items and spaces that are spilling over. But before we get into any of those, we start with that space between our ears. Once we get clarity here, those other solutions come more easily. We build on the progress, and it gets exciting. For now, let this simply serve as permission to get moving and maybe even enjoy the productivity of creating a well-ordered home.

Tip: There are times when I spend the first few minutes with a guest chatting while casually tidying up the most impactful areas, such as moving dirty dishes to the sink and picking up kids' jackets from the floor to the coat hooks. For me personally, I can enjoy my visitors so much more if I've done those quick tasks.

Discovering Our Truest Interest

Like most epiphanies, when we shine light on them, they seem so obvious, yet until we do, there they are in the background, subtly pulling us in one direction or another. So it was with our old bath mats that had long since lost their memory foam cushion. Every time I saw them, I felt disappointed. It felt like scarcity, like settling, so when I would walk into the master bathroom, it didn't feel good. Finally, one day, after talking with an amazing designer named Megan Vukich, who has a passion for creating homes with a beautiful ambience, I got the nudge I needed to let the mats go. I decided to give them away instead of just trashing them because the seams are all still fresh, and someone out there may need them.

For a week or two, I had no bath mats at all, and that actually felt better. Like a blank canvas, it felt more like an opportunity instead of settling and being stuck. It felt more like curiosity and would gently lead my mind into a space of asking, "What DO I want?" I pondered it in my heart.

That was not an easy question to answer. One day, I thought of deep bluish-green mats in the room since that is a color I've enjoyed since childhood that has come back into fashion lately. That led me down a path of feeling the need to refinish the cabinets, maybe even replace the cabinet doors, and to add pops of the same matching color into other places in the bathroom with new decor. It felt like a growing project as I thought about the timeline and cost, contractors and bids, shopping and coordinating. It didn't feel like peace. It didn't feel quite right. And I couldn't quite picture an image in my mind that seemed like what I dreamed of.

Then I found what I truly wanted. It seems that it was there all along, but I didn't have the courage to be that authentic yet. What I really wanted were oversized, plush, white bath mats that are soft under our feet. It seemed impractical to walk on white and might show dirt right away. At first, when I discovered that desire, it felt a little scary. Then, as I imagined white mats in the space while standing in the master bathroom, it all seemed so simple. There were already white elements in the bathroom, so nothing else would need to change. As I rested in this new idea, peace came. The resolve grew.

I found those plush, oversized, white bath mats in the luxury hotel line at Walmart for $20 each. Because of the size, it only took two—one for each sink—for the bathroom to feel complete. There didn't even need to be one in front of the bathtub or shower.

Now that they're in our home, it would be easy to forget that it was a process at all. How hard could it be to get a couple of white bath mats, right? But I haven't forgotten the work it takes to be true to who we are, to discover our true wants, to step into who we were made to be, and to walk in that truth. Benjamin Franklin used to say this every day:

"O powerful goodness! Bountiful Father! Merciful Guide! Increase in me that wisdom which discovers my truest interest. Strengthen my resolution to perform what that wisdom dictates. Accept my kind offices to thy other children as the only return in my power for thy continual favours to me."

Megan Vukich, a talented interior designer who takes the time to understand her clients and help create the home they want, challenged me to find bath mats that I really love. She reminded me that it's a small decision since it's easy to change, but that it has a big impact. If I ended up hating how the mats looked in our space, I would just return them! She also encouraged me to be confident in what I love and in my expression of what I want to put in our space and in our home. She invited me to dabble with it. She said you'll slowly start gaining confidence as you get that item and then have the "Oh, I love this!" feeling.

Megan believes our home is a safe haven. It's the place where we experience our highest highs and lowest lows. Having a space that you feel is yours, that you love, that you want to come home to and be in, changes the whole feel. It's your sanctuary, a place of refuge and safety. Even though it's just material things, when you love all those things, it's almost like baggage is lifted off of you. It's just great.

What is a room telling you?

For me, when I take one to two minutes in the morning to make my bed, it sends a message to my brain that I'm okay, I'm handling it, and I'm not overwhelmed. Every time throughout the day that I walk back into the room, it's a reminder of those messages.

However, there are days—maybe if I was up with the baby several times the night before or am fighting a sickness—when an unmade bed says, "today is a good day for a nap." It gives me permission to slow down, be kind to myself, and take the breaks that make sense today. On those days, when I see the unmade bed, it says rest is coming, and today is a day to be gentle with myself.

If toys are out, does it say, "kids are welcome here?" Sometimes we will intentionally leave the couch set up as a fort for the kids for a day or two, even though it takes over the entire living room, because it is such a fun reminder of the gift and joy of these kids. For me, as long as there's a limit in my mind of when it will all be put away, the message it sends to me is that I'm a fun mom and that this home is my kids' home too. There have been times when the message it sent me was that the kids were taking over the house and we were living in chaos, but as I've become more aware of these subtle messages, it has also shown how we often get to choose those messages. Does the blank wall say that our home isn't done, or does it say that we have the patience and discernment to wait for the right item to come along?

The old bath mats said all the wrong things to me. Pay attention to how you feel in a room, and then if there's something that doesn't sit right, gently and patiently start to ask why. As you go through this book, more and more ideas will surface that help identify what that might be. We'll also help you troubleshoot some design elements that can make a room feel off but that we may not notice as the cause. For example, our master bedroom felt like the worst room in the house for my husband and me until my cousin with a design eye pointed out the clashing metals that we hadn't noticed.

How do I change what a room is telling me?

There are two solutions:

Exercise

1.   Rethink it.

Choose a space in your home that doesn't feel like you want it too yet. What is the message that space is sending you, or what is it you think or feel about it?

____

____

Good! Sometimes even just saying or writing the thought or feeling brings it to the conscious level, and sometimes when we hear it or see it written, it starts to change (or we consciously realize we don't agree, at least not entirely). Now that you've identified the thought or feeling, if it isn't serving you, what do you want to think or feel instead?

____

____

Are you able to make the switch from the thought that isn't serving you to the new one?

Yes or No

Test it: when I offer my brain a new thought or feeling, I'll ask myself, "is that true?" or "do I believe it?" Usually, my brain gives me a yes or no. This helps me bounce the idea back and forth and see if it resonates. Then if it doesn't, pick a different one!

Tip: If the new thought, such as "this is a beautiful space," doesn't quite feel true, try adding an anchor at the beginning, like "I am becoming" a person who creates beautiful spaces or "this room is well on its way to being lovely and just needs a few more touches." Sometimes softening the comment a bit with "this is becoming" allows us to accept a much better thought.

Even if getting this space to where you want it to be is going to take more than thought work, this is still such a great place to start. This identifies for you the problem and what you want to change. Sometimes all that needs to change is a thought process. Either way, if it's more than that, this brings clarity and focus, which brings us to our next solution...

2. Physically change something in the room.

For Mother's Day this year, we got a gorgeous and still modestly priced couple of wooden chairs and a little wooden table that we came across while we were out together. Even when we don't sit in them and I just drive by or walk in, every time I set eyes on that gorgeous wood, it brings me a little burst of joy! Sometimes making a change, taking something out that's cluttering the space, swapping a few pieces around, putting new covers on the throw pillows, or making bigger changes makes a difference.

Another simple example was in an apartment that we called home for a month. Do you know what made it home for me? I simply put a Polaroid family picture on the refrigerator with a magnetic clip. Done. For some reason, that tiny picture in the center of the fridge made me breathe out a sigh of relief and feel like this was our home. The Murphy family picture stayed on the fridge until the day we moved out, and even removing it held this pleasant significance of the ending of this small season of life.

Keeping up with the Joneses

We literally live across the street from the Joneses. Isn't it a perfect analogy for how it feels to try to keep up with the neighbors or make decisions about our home from a place of comparison instead of contentment and joy? How would we ever keep up?

How easy is it to slip into that unhealthy headspace of wanting my home to be beautiful because of the neighbors? Every time my mind goes there, it robs me of my joy. It also zaps my creativity and courage. My space starts to become boring and "safe" so that "everyone" will approve of it and like it. But we each have different tastes. We each have pieces that are meaningful to us for different reasons. We each have different family histories and heirlooms to display. There are nuances to each of our styles and stories.

The truth is, when you create a space that is uniquely your own, that resonates with you, you will feel more comfortable in your skin, regardless of the reactions from visitors. After all, it's you, and not the visitors, who live there. My hope and prayer is that when people visit our home, they will be inspired to be comfortable in their own unique space, to fully embody who God made them to be, and will leave with renewed energy instead of a draining emotion like envy.

Breaking Free of the Comparison Trap

My friend Amy and her mom, Mary Beth, both have such beautiful homes, and yet when they came over, they loved our home and readily admitted to several aspects of their homes that they would prefer to change. They complimented the floor plan because of what it offered that their homes didn't. The irony of it was that I was nervous for days leading up to the visit, feeling self-conscious about my own home and comparing it to theirs in my mind. As we visited together in my living room, I realized that even with each of their incredible homes, no home is perfect. If we're waiting for that, it's elusive and will not come. We can be happy, satisfied, and at rest in our homes now, with whatever they do and don't offer, even while we dream and work towards something.

For some reason, that visit was so freeing. Being asked several times if we felt "settled" in our home suddenly made me realize I can and should. Seeing our home through the eyes of our lovely guests was refreshing because, to them, it looked settled and homey. Suddenly, the ideas and dreams I still have left for our home became fun and exciting. I can view them as gradual, OPTIONAL additions, not as necessary pieces that leave us living in the future. We can have that now, even if it's sitting on the floor in a spot where we imagine one day having a comfy chair or looking at a bare wall that we picture one day being adorned with meaningful art pieces.

The antidote to the comparison trap is two-fold. First, the more we can be true to who we are, the smaller the comparison becomes in our minds. No one else is trying to be the best "Maya Murphy" they can be. I'm the only one. You're the only [insert your name here]. So, if we're not competing to be the same person, if our callings, missions, tastes, and preferences are as unique as our fingerprints, then there is no competition. And if there is no competition, what is there to compare?

Second, so often, the comparison comes from the feeling that someone else has something we want. If they have something we want, and we have the resources to get it, and it truly is something that we believe will bring us joy, go get one. Comparison over. If it's not really something we want or need, or isn't something we're in a position to have right now, then, my friends, it's simply envy. That's a joy-killer. Like being bitten by a snake, it poisons us from the inside out. Thank God there is a remedy.

The antidote to envy is gratitude. I'm not talking about some intangible, warm, fuzzy buzzword. We can train our hearts and minds to bend towards gratitude, and when we do, we will see our homes in an entirely different light and will truly enjoy them. If you have basic comforts and shelter, your home is better equipped than billions of people on earth. Even that statement can be taken two ways: we can feel bad that others are in need, or we can be grateful for our blessings and do our small part to help those less fortunate.

As we teach our minds to live in gratitude, over time it becomes easier and easier. Eventually, gratitude becomes our default mode. The more that happens, the more abundant life feels. Isn't that a comforting way to enjoy our homes?

On Making Decisions

Prioritizing

We learned to prioritize the hard way. We paved the side yard for RV parking before getting a bigger dining table. That's okay. A wise man once told me that if you survive your education, you're doing alright.

One day, on a walk around the block with the kids, we made a list, in order, of what we wanted most for our home. Now, as new ideas come up, we can bounce them against our list of what is most important to us. Let's be real: a lot of times, ideas come up randomly or because of great marketing! This list is helping us remember that we better make good on the rock climbing wall we've been telling our kiddo we would put in his room before paving the side yard for RV parking. In our case, unfortunately we did those in reverse order before we made our list. Now we've made good on our promises.

Rock climbing wall as promised

Comfort Over Comparison

One idea that I continue to discern is whether I'm choosing elements for our home because they're impressive or because they're homey. Years ago, we looked at an impressive tight leather couch. But when we sat in it, while it looked crisp, it didn't have much give and wasn't very comfortable. It was stiff and elegant. Then we sat on a different couch with a softer material and a shape that you fell into a little more. It didn't have the dignified look of the first one, but it was cozy. Over the years, we have enjoyed many family movie nights on our comfy couch. We've wiped many spills off this workhorse piece of furniture. Popcorn has been eaten, spilled, and cleaned out of the creases. Naps have happened more times than I could count.

For me, I can feel the difference in my body when I ask whether I'm choosing this for comfort or comparison. For example, we recently looked at some beautiful options for flowers. I liked them both and felt torn. Then, when I checked in with myself and paid attention to how each made me feel, I noticed a stark contrast. One color choice made me feel stimulated, impressed, awake, and like I had just drunk a cup of coffee. The other color choice made my whole body go "aaah." My shoulders relaxed and dropped as I took a deep breath in and out. For me, the latter is what I want to feel as I pull into the driveway at home or walk into my backyard. I want to feel like it's time to lay my troubles down. It feels like peace, and that's a great feeling to work and live from. The more I select items that feel like "aaah," the more my home convinces my heart, mind, and body to have peace and be me.

High Stakes and Low Stakes Decisions

Another foundational piece I want to discuss early on is differentiating between high-stakes and low-stakes decisions. Items that are inexpensive and easy to return or swap out are low-stakes. The bathmats were a low-stakes decision, but I didn't know that for a long time. It kept me from giving myself permission to just try something out! That's harder to do with kitchen cabinets, for example, but in today's world, there are lots of ways to see items in our space for those bigger-ticket items, so you get to test-drive them before you decide.

Being able to label something as a "low-stakes decision" takes the pressure off. It brings a sigh of relief and permission to explore. Until this idea came up, my brain liked to make everything a high-stakes decision, but that's simply not true. Really, very few decisions in life are truly high-stakes. Paint can be changed, pillows are a big pop and bang for your buck and are a super simple swap, and light fixtures have a big impact on a room in a fairly small amount of time and cost. Let's not put pressure on those little decisions and let them be fun and easy.

Lowering the Stakes on Bigger Decisions

You don't have to do all of these. In fact, you don't have to do any of these. I'm sharing ideas that have come up along the way to help you get comfortable with design decisions. I also know people who have put together different pieces—maybe all the elements that were on sale, for example—and then loved how it all came together without these tips. But if you're wanting a little help to move forward on a couch or bigger item, or if you're changing several items and want to make sure they'll go together, these are some design tips to try.

1. Get samples of all the elements you're considering and hold them together. For example, in a kitchen this might be a paint swatch, a piece of flooring, a sample countertop piece, a cabinet door, and the cabinet handle. Leave them in the space for a little time so you see them in different lighting and so you see them as you walk in and out of the room when you're not thinking about it. When you walk in and see these pieces together, what's your gut reaction? And if there's one you don't like, it's super easy to swap it out to try a different one. We did this with our kitchen, and the pieces that I loved when I walked back in the room are still the pieces I love today. It's an easy way to test drive an idea and see what resonates with you. This also helps with selecting items that work well together.

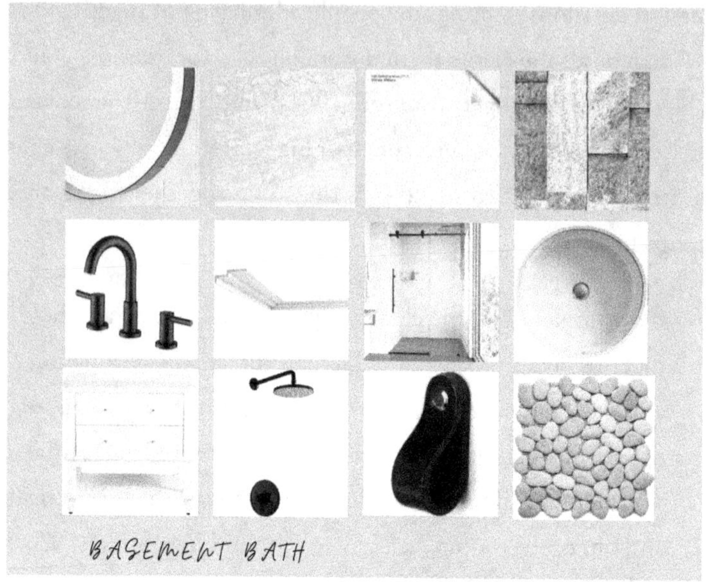

Basement Bath Elements

2. Another option is to snap a picture of the room you're considering changing (without even picking up every little item that's out of place because let's keep it real y'all) and drop an image of the item(s) you're considering into the picture. You should be able to see what it looks like. What do you think?

3. Sometimes the best ideas happen on the "back of a napkin" because we keep it simple. Try drawing the living space on a piece of paper. This option goes well with getting sample pieces in tip #1 since this lets you imagine the layout and what you would do in the space while tip #1 lets you see the decor items.

4. Especially if you like variety, one way to lower the stakes on the bigger ticket items is by allowing the more expensive pieces to be more neutral and timeless so the pillows and throw blankets, bathmats and small decor items bring in the seasonal elements, modern touches, and pops of color. You don't have to do this

though. If you want a space to be more stimulating, exciting, arousing and energizing, a bold couch or rug goes a long way!

Strengthening the Decision Muscle

We can stagnate on decisions, but like any muscle, the more we work it, the stronger it gets. One key piece is: what state of mind are we in when we're trying to decide? Are you feeling strong, confident, empowered, and peaceful? Are you feeling fearful? Are you in a place of comparison?

Before deciding, pause and check your mood. If you feel fear or overwhelm, stand up, shake it out, jump up and down a few times, and even make a funny noise like "gobble gobble gobble" or "weeoo weeoo"—this physical shift helps your brain release stress hormones and regain clarity (Tony Robbins calls this 'physiology first'). Then stand tall and ask yourself: "What do I really want?" or "What feels true to me?"

The Joy of Being Bold

Being bold comes with risk, and risk, by definition, means it may or may not work out. But without an element of uncertainty, I don't even think we can feel alive. It's an irreplaceable ingredient to having adventures. It's one of the elements that makes our life exciting. We can and should weigh our risks against the rewards to make thoughtful decisions about which risks are worth taking on, which ones make sense for us, and which ones may be out of balance.

So how does this apply to making our house a home? I think it's because it takes courage to do something bold in our own space. And really, if we're going to create a space that reflects who we are, every one of us is unique in our likes, preferences, stories, memories, and families. This is what empowers us to make a space we love. This is what grounds us. This also gives us permission to make mistakes along the way and change it later! We can give ourselves permission to try it out and take it back if it ends up not working.

I can let myself try that style that really might be what I like. Doesn't it sound liberating?

Friend, it is worth it. Along the way, we also discover more of who we are, even with the pieces we don't end up liking, so they all work together for our good. The days when I take that risk and feel like I'm in my own skin are the days when I feel fully alive. Isn't it inspiring to imagine a home space that brings you back into that truer, braver version of yourself? Then we have somewhere that helps bring out our most authentic selves more and more. Then we have somewhere we can be free.

For Couples: Unity and Compromise

The "compromises" in our home between my husband Dave and I have become one of my most loved aspects. For the first several years, it felt like the aspects he brought into our home just took away the parts I wanted, made our home less of me, and felt a bit like the sand left in your swimsuit after a day at the beach. Now though, the parts that are important to him have become important to me because I want him to enjoy our home and feel like it's his just as much as I want to feel like it's mine.

Our home tells our story. The blend of our styles in our home has become this visible reminder of the blend of our lives in marriage, the miracle of the covenant of marriage when two people become one in the eyes of God. And over the last ten years, I've come to appreciate the parts of his style that hadn't been mine at first. For example, he likes traditional style. For me, this used to be boring. But now, I've come to appreciate how aspects of traditional style are timeless. They're tried and true. In fact, what started out as something I didn't like but tolerated for him has become something I like for what it is too.

Are we still drawn to different things? Yes sometimes. I tend to like a rustic style more than he does, and he still likes a traditional style more than me. We both like some modern elements. That works well because you can have up to 3 styles in a home while still looking intentional and cohesive. So we have one style we both chose (modern), and then each of us added one more style (rustic for me and traditional for him). We've learned, and continue to learn, how to recognize those elements that are most important to each of us, to let go of those that matter less, to communicate those preferences with each other, and to end up with something that keeps each of our favorites.

Allow yourself to like what you like and assertively stand up for what matters most to you. At the same time, find joy in seeing your significant other reflected in the home you create together. This blend can tell your shared story and create a home that brings you even closer together.

Making a House a Home is a Process, Not an Event.

Like diet and exercise, making a house a home is a lifestyle. It's okay for spaces to adapt over time in both function and fashion. This happens naturally as we go through life and as items wear out. It can still serve you and be your home all along the way

If you're anything like me, this idea might bring on two feelings at the same time. One of those is perhaps a little disappointment. At first I thought this was something I could finish and check off my to do list. To realize this is an ongoing task like dishes and laundry at first felt like a burden. But equally strong was this feeling of relief. I don't have to get it all figured out and done all at once. It's not a task with a crazy timeline. There is time to let things simmer and let ideas come up organically, to let this develop into what serves us best at different times. It's also exciting to get to change it around and freshen it up if and when I want.

Think it Through and Enjoy it for Years.

Sometimes decisions happen quickly and from the gut. Those are amazing! Sometimes we just know we love something, go for it, and never look back. Other times, there's a little bit of a process to think through the steps. When we were planning our kitchen remodel, a piece of advice we were given was to think about what we would keep in our kitchen and where we would store it so that we could design the cabinets and drawers to support how we live in our space.

That ended up being well worth it. I took about an hour to think about where we would store each of our kitchen items. I decided where to keep plates, bowls, cups, and silverware based on where the sink and dishwasher were located in particular. Since we knew where we wanted to store them, I was able to order the silverware insert for the drawer that came from the cabinet company, so it fits perfectly. It also makes unloading a breeze since those cabinets are all right next to the dishwasher. We have a cupboard with cups up top, then the silverware drawer, then a deep drawer big enough for bowls and plates, and on the bottom, a kids' drawer where they can reach their own plastic plates and cups (one day this will be our outdoor plastic plates since it's closest to the back doors).

I only had to do this once for about an hour, and for years we have been reaping the benefits of thinking it through in a space that we use every day. This is so worth it! What a valuable use of a little bit of time and work.

Key Takeaways

- Focusing on what you personally like, rather than what's trendy or expected, creates a truly fulfilling home. You are allowed to like what is trendy and expected too.

- Distinguish between "comfort" and "comparison" in your home choices; prioritize what brings genuine ease and joy, not what you think will impress others.

- Making decisions about your home is a skill that can be strengthened with practice. Differentiating between "high stakes" and "low stakes" decisions reduces pressure and encourages experimentation.

- Your home should serve you, not the other way around; find a balance between upkeep and relaxation, and give yourself permission to enjoy your space as it is.

Chapter 4

Planning Your Resources

Financial stewardship transforms lives. I've seen how it reduces stress, improves sleep, and strengthens relationships. As someone with a business degree and experience managing multi-million dollar project finances, I bring these lessons here to help you build your home on a solid financial foundation. It's not necessarily sexy, and rarely do people see it, but everything else is built on it. It's worth doing right.

When the financial picture is aligned with God's guidance, it builds our home on a foundation of financial peace and joy. When it's built on debt and overspending, it damages relationships and is a foundation with cracks in it. Money problems are among the top five leading causes of divorce. That's not a foundation for a home that reflects the people living in it, that's functional, or that's beautiful. That doesn't feel good, no matter what the cabinets look like. It isn't rightly ordered when we prioritize things over our own peace and relationships.

The good news is that home isn't a price point. After all you've read in this book so far, I hope that's clear, and we will only continue to build on that principle. In this chapter, I'll teach you how to build your home on a solid financial foundation so that it stands strong, weathers the storms, brings

75

peace, and facilitates greater connections in your relationships and with yourself. And we'll keep it super simple, so you don't have to be a nerd like me to do it!

Exercise

Before we get into the details of managing your resources, let's take a step back and build a framework for the conversation. This chapter is mainly about HOW to plan out the resources for your home. We can sometimes get bogged down in it, but not when we're rooted in what we want and why we want it. Take a couple of minutes to do this, and it will make this whole chapter flow so much better. This short, easy exercise will give you momentum by rooting you in what you're creating and <u>why</u> it's worth it to you to do this.

1. When it comes to your home, what do you want? [What do you want it to feel like? This is a space to dream and have fun with it. Example: I want a beautiful space that serves me and the people living in it. I want it to be a reflection of who we are and to energize us, to be functional and easy to use. I want it to be gorgeous and rustic so it inspires me and makes me feel true to who I am].__________________

____

____

2. Great! Well done. Why do you want that for your home? [What will life be like once it's this way? How will you feel? What will you think of it? Example: We spend so much time in our home, I want it to be one of my favorite places in the world.] _______

____

____

> 3. Nice! Now that you're rooted in what you want and why, it's so much easier to figure out how to get there. And you're set up for success in getting to the end that you truly want!
>
> **Tip:** This is an exercise that you can come back to over and over. First, answer these questions at a high level, thinking about overall what you want for your home. Then, you can answer it for specific rooms or projects or areas to help hone in on what you want to do in that space, what you want it to feel like, and how you want it to serve you.

Budget

Being house poor isn't homey. I don't think a house feels like a home if it's out of our price range, if there's financial stress from being stretched, and if looking at the beautiful elements around us is a constant reminder of what we have but cannot afford. A high end contractor named Andre who did some consulting work for us once told me, "I've been in very expensive houses that were not homes, and I've been in cozy little houses that were homes." Blowing our budget and living beyond our means is about the fastest way to not feel at home in our space, and that's why I come here next. A remodel can be done at a wide variety of price ranges. We can do simple things on a budget that have a big impact.

Here are a few examples:

*Fresh paint
*Updated hardware on cabinets and doors
*Visible family photos
* Meaningful decor or heirlooms
*Adding plants
*Rearranging or repurposing existing items (shopping your own home)
*Decluttering

There will be more tips and ideas for those in the chapters to come. Before we go deep into remodeling ideas, start with this brief exercise to assess your financial situation.

1. First, count your cash.

What Money is There Now?

Current balance in bank account(s)	+
Cash in other accounts (investments, etc.)	+
Total Cash now:	=

2. Great! There are usually high points and low points in the month where bank balances go up and down as bills and income hit, and we don't want to spend cash that's already committed to something else. So now let's look out over the next 30 days at what will be coming. First, let's look at what money is expected to come in:

What Money is Coming in the Next 30 Days?

Regular Income	+
Investment Income (interest, rents, etc)	+
Other Income: (child support, tax refund, etc.)	+
Total Income expected	=

Tip: A great way to gather this information is to look back over the last month or few months to see what hit the bank account. Also check back far enough to catch income/expenses that may only happen every 6 months or year. For example, some insurance bills are only charged once or twice a year, depending on how you set them up.

3. Nice! Now we'll estimate what money will be coming out over the next month. Is there a credit card bill, mortgage, rent payment, utilities, and other bills that will come out of the bank account? Are there any other financial commitments that have already been made but not paid yet?

What Money is Going Out in the Next 30 Days?

Tithe/Donations	-
Mortgage or Rent payment	-
Credit card payment	-
Utility bills	-
Loan payments (Student loans, HELOC, etc)	-
Home or renters Insurance	-
Car Insurance	-
Health Insurance	-
Life Insurance	-
Car payment	-
Fuel and vehicle maintenance	-
Food expenses	-

Toiletries	-
School/work expenses	-
Clothing	-
Subscriptions:	-
Other expense:	-
Other expense:	-
Other expense:	-
Total Expenses Expected	=

4. That was a big one! Congrats, because you have now gathered up the information you need to build a budget, if you don't already have one. This is huge! Now let's put these pieces from 1-3 together.

Totals

1. Total Cash Now	+
2. Total Income Expected	+
Subtotal (Cash Now + Income Expected)	=
3. Total Expenses Expected	-
4. What the balance will be	=

Example: If the bank account has $10 in it now + $5 in income expected (=$15) - $7 in expenses expected = $8 is what the balance should be soon.

If you just got paid and all the bills are about to hit, it would be easy to overestimate how much cash is available without going through this little exercise. I do this whenever we're considering a bigger purchase or whenever we want to get a snapshot on our money. It gets quicker and easier each time. At this point, it only takes a few minutes, and it sure keeps me out of trouble! This is how we make sure we're not spending money that's already committed to something else.

Why is this important? Can't we just put it on a credit card, or take out a loan, and worry about it later?

Proverbs 22:7 says "…the borrower is servant to the lender." There is no reason to become a slave remodeling a house. This isn't necessary to have a home. Be free. Pay cash or wait.

Borrower is slave

We are reminded again when Paul tells us in Romans 13:8, "Let no debt remain outstanding, except the continuing debt to love one another…" What's fun is that when we start from this solid, biblical foundation, then we open our minds to be able to think of creative and economical ways to create the home we want. It becomes a challenge and an adventure. It can even be a game, like playing real life Monopoly, and it is so fun to win the money game! In this game, no one has to lose either. There's no reason to break the bank. There is not an income level where financial freedom stops mattering. The number of zeroes might change ($200. $200,000), but the principles are the same.

Maybe you are in a solid financial position and are ready to make major financial investments in your home. If that's you, congratulations and enjoy the fruits of your labor! If you're not there yet, don't sweat it. You can still create home…

Small homey touches

And with that, let's keep going! Now let's get into where to prioritize remodel expenses.

Christian financial guru Dave Ramsey has worked since 1992 helping people manage their money the way God says to in His word. There are many millionaires today, many people out of debt, and many people experiencing financial peace all over the country because of his simple and easy-to-apply methods for managing money. There's no need to reinvent the wheel, so I'll share how he teaches these Biblical principles.

Some criticize these techniques as being too simple. I know because that used to be me. We thought we were too financially sophisticated and mature for his methods, but he didn't invent them; they came straight out of the Bible. What I was really saying, without knowing it, is that I thought I knew better than God. Dave Ramsey said to "move at the speed of cash." It may feel slow at first, but you will be blown away by how quickly it progresses. You won't believe how good it feels because it's right. It's amazing how much money you can keep and save just by prioritizing it. Most of all, the financial peace it brings is life-giving.

Dave Ramsey breaks it down into 7 baby steps:[1]

1. Save $1,000 for Your Starter Emergency Fund
2. Pay Off All Debt (Except the House) Using the Debt Snowball (pay off the smallest debt first and then snowball that amount onto the 2nd smallest debt, etc.)
3. Save 3–6 Months of Expenses in a Fully Funded Emergency Fund
4. 3b. Save a down payment for your home (if you don't have one yet)
5. Invest 15% of Your Household Income in Retirement
6. Save for Your Children's College Fund
7. Pay Off Your Home Early
8. Build Wealth and Give. As he puts it, "Live like no one else so later you can live and give like no one else."

Having a $1,000 emergency fund means not having to rely on a credit card for every little hiccup. That's life-changing and shifts how money is used.

---

1   Dave Ramsey, "The 7 Baby Steps," Ramsey Solutions, accessed July 4, 2024, https://www.ramseysolutions.com/dave-ramsey-7-baby-steps.

Albert Einstein said that compound interest is the 8th wonder of the world. Money can snowball in a good way, using compound interest to build wealth in your sleep while your money makes more money, or it can be just as powerful in a bad way, paying interest on interest and making it harder to dig out of a hole. Paying off the debt is huge.

Having a fully funded emergency fund brings peace of mind, gives options, and brings freedom. This keeps people on solid financial ground even with life's bigger setbacks.

The later seasons of life are coming whether we're prepared for them or not. Time is a powerful ally, and small amounts invested early pay huge dividends when they're compounded over decades. This is too important to ignore. Making budget-friendly decisions for our homes is well worth it to prioritize being prepared for retirement. This brings peace by being rightly ordered.

Likewise, for anyone with children, there are great options, like a 529 plan, that offer big tax savings for those who are willing to plan ahead. This is another powerful way to get the financial snowball working in your direction since the earnings compound (remember Einstein's quote about the 8th wonder of the world). Put in small amounts consistently over time, and the easiest way to do this is to set it on autopay. Within a 529 plan, those investments grow tax-free and can be pulled out tax-free as long as they're used for qualifying education expenses like tuition, books, or room and board. Fashions and home styles change, but being prepared for your children's future doesn't go out of style.

I have yet to meet someone with a paid-off house who wishes they had a mortgage! Having financial peace in your home will improve your life more than a doodad or item you may buy. These principles are only daunting until we make the decision to follow them, and then even while we're working at it, the progress makes it incredibly rewarding.

What good does it do to have the most beautiful couch in the neighborhood if you'll be on the street at age 65? When we challenge ourselves to be more creative financially, we find solutions we had previously overlooked. I also find it thrilling to get a good deal! One small, recent example is a rocking chair we were wanting to purchase. I found a beautiful, quality chair at Pottery Barn that would cost about $2,000 by the time it was delivered. Before pulling the trigger, I searched a couple of used websites and found a Pottery Barn chair for sale locally for $350. Winning!

I understand that for some, this may feel like a cold shower. If it does, let's call it a renewal and a cleansing, perhaps even a baptism of sorts. Do the hard work to live a good, abundant life that's rooted and correctly ordered. You will love who it helps you become and the freedom it gives you. Seriously, y'all, what's a new kitchen if you're drowning in debt? How will the four walls around us bring us peace if we've built them on a rocky financial foundation? And how will we find the satisfaction only God can bring if we don't listen to Him?

If we had not saved up the cash, instead of gutting the kitchen, I would have added some simple open shelves on a spot of wall that was bare, added some cute decorative elements for the shelves (most likely a mix of existing items, family treasures, and perhaps a couple of small new pieces of decor to tie it all together), gotten a nice bowl for the center of the island, and replaced some of the hinges on the cabinets that no longer closed smoothly.

If we still had a couple of hundred dollars, I probably would have measured the distance between the screw holes on the existing cabinet pulls and replaced them with new handles with the same distance between the screws. The new ones could even look bigger if they extended beyond where they screwed into the cabinets. If we had a couple of thousand dollars available, the next item on the wish list would have been replacing the appliances, which could have waited for a Black Friday or Memorial Day sale (or a good secondhand find!). These examples show how we can freshen and personalize our homes at different price points.

Tip: One caveat here is a reminder to differentiate between necessary home maintenance, fixing items that prevent the home from getting damaged like repairing or replacing the roof, and upgrades, like prettier kitchen cabinets. Repairs and routine maintenance are simply one of the expenses of owning a home, much like a utility payment, so we include these in the budget.

Things are Not Always What They Seem

We were just finishing touring their 6,000-square-foot custom home. They'd shown us all three levels, and now we were on their private master bedroom deck with sweeping views. We started talking about money, and then he said, "We're house poor." I was surprised by the statement since they seemed so wealthy. He and his wife both had six-figure jobs, their kids were in private schools, they drove nice cars, and they lived in an absolute dream home with 300-degree views.

But with that small, simple comment, the underlying circumstances were revealed. What looked so glamorous from the outside wasn't supported as much as it seemed. Robert Kiyosaki, an American businessman and author known for the influential book "Rich Dad Poor Dad," says, "It's not how much you make, it's how much you keep." So even with plenty of income flowing in, that money flowed right back out. They were living large, but no wealth was being created for all the work they were doing. And I wonder, how much were they really enjoying it knowing that they had to pick up extra work trips to continue supporting the lavish lifestyle?

This is why I put the chapter on resources before talking about all the pretty things and the design. This comes first because it is foundational. It matters to prioritize and plan the resources, and starting here does just that. Make sure you can comfortably afford it, not just barely. Leave margin, which means having money left in the bank. It's not necessary for a home to stretch yourself thin financially.

If this is overwhelming at all, take heart! I bet if you look back at your life at the hardest things you've done, they've also been the most rewarding. You are reading this book, taking the time to improve your life and home, and that sets you apart. You're already one of the few. You're already one of the great ones. Play that all the way through and do this right, because that's who you truly are and who you're made to be. You've got this, and this is worth it. Root back to what you want and why you want it, because this work is creating the life of your dreams. That's not a life with a beautiful kitchen and an empty bank account; your life is one of abundance.

Exercise

If you don't have a budget yet, STOP! Flip to Appendix A and use the template to create your budget (your money plan). You've already done most of the legwork with the exercise earlier in this chapter to count your cash, and you will feel amazing when you're done!

Remember, there are lots of ways to make your home more homey that don't have to break the bank, and for those other areas, you get to play the game of swapping out your latte or other optional costs to redirect and free up the money for your home. This can be a fun challenge and exciting endeavor. This is a good life.

Tip: Remember we can always change our perspective to make our homes feel amazing. For example, if you've been dreaming of a new couch and are now taking care of financial priorities first, every time you look at that old couch, you can tell yourself, "I am a person who makes amazing decisions. I have self-discipline, and I'm intentional with my resources. I'm enjoying what we have now and looking forward to what we will one day enjoy at the same time."

Counting the Cost

The Bible reminds us of the importance of planning before starting a project. Luke 14:28 says, "Suppose one of you wants to build a tower. Will he not first sit down and estimate the cost to see if he has enough money to complete it? For if he lays the foundation and is not able to finish it, everyone who sees it will ridicule him, saying, 'This fellow began to build and was not able to finish.'"

Budget Tip for Homeowners

It's prudent to include 10% of your monthly payment toward repairs and maintenance. Three years could go by without any repairs needed, and then an expensive repair occurs, such as needing a new roof or furnace. However, even that kind of expense doesn't have to be a surprise. If you own your home, take whatever your mortgage payment is (or whatever a reasonable payment on your home would be) and figure that 10% of that amount is a good average for maintenance overall. If the home is a 100-year-old Craftsman or has more than normal deferred maintenance, you may want to plan for a little more. For example, if the mortgage payment is $1,500/month, then $1,500 x 10% = $150/month should be budgeted toward repairs and maintenance. So, in a month with no repairs needed, you should see a savings of $150, meaning the bank account should grow by that amount. Learn the financial maturity to not spend it and rather to earmark it, at least in your mind, for future maintenance and repairs that will come. This will give you peace of mind. This will help your house feel like a home. This will bring more quality of life than the vacation or toy that could be bought with that money, leaving no nest egg for when the repairs come. Repairs don't have to be scary, intimidating, or unplanned. You may not know exactly what they will be and when they will be needed, but we do know they are a part of having a home. If we manage our expectations well in this area, life will be easier and more enjoyable. Disneyland isn't nearly as much fun when we're worried about a water heater back at home!

Another good rule of thumb cited by NerdWallet, Investopedia, and several other sources is to set aside 1% of your home value each year for repairs and maintenance (and even as high as 4% depending on the age and condition of the home). That means if your home is worth $300,000, at 1%, you can expect to spend $3,000 a year on maintenance, which comes out to $250 a month. Remember again that while you may not have any maintenance costs for several months or longer, there may be a larger expense item like windows needed, so it's still prudent to set that money aside. These expenses don't wait like the optional upgrades. Oftentimes, neglecting inexpensive routine maintenance items, like new caulk around windows or the bathtub, will lead to much bigger expenses in the long run as damage is caused. This rule of thumb is nice since it isn't affected by the interest rate of the mortgage or by fluctuating rents.

Exercise

Which one of these calculations works best for you? 10% of payment or 1% of home value

Option 1: Monthly Payment x 10% = ____________________

Option 2: Home Value x 1% = ___________ / 12 months = _____________

Now flip to the Budget in Appendix A. Put in that $ amount for Housing - Home Maintenance

---

Generosity with Ourselves, Our Family, and Others

I greatly admire those generous souls like Mother Teresa. She took a vow of poverty and said because she chose to live life in that way, she was financially free. She wasn't a victim of her circumstances, but rather she chose to both live free of the temptation that comes with money and to live free of the burden of poverty that could come from it being the only option available.

I've learned more about money from this impoverished nun than I would have thought possible, because until I listened to her, I didn't realize financial "freedom" could look this way. She relied on Divine Providence for her every need, and not once in her lifetime did God disappoint. Whoever came in her path needing help, she helped, and not once was the supply too short to help those before her. She made me realize that many people who have achieved great wealth are not actually free because if they don't trust, they still live in financial fear. So where do we put our trust and our faith? Is it in our money or our home or our possessions? To whatever degree our faith is in those items, we are not free. And to whatever degree our faith is truly rooted in our Lord and Savior, we are free.

Open Hands

There's a posture with which we can approach God and our lives: open hands. To help bring meaning to this phrase, I'll explain the other postures we could choose instead. One is a clenched fist, saying, "I will keep this no matter what. You can't have it. I don't trust you with it. I won't give it up." This comes from not trusting God or others and thinking that if we open our hands to them, it will be worse. The fear is that something will be taken from us, or something will be placed upon us that will make our lives worse.

On the other end of the spectrum, we can use our hands to push away that which we don't feel we deserve. This one can be sneaky! This comes from not trusting ourselves. We feel unworthy; we think we won't be a good steward or manager of it. We think someone else needs it more or deserves it more or will handle it better. This one is subtle, because it's almost a knee-jerk reaction. This is how we rob ourselves of the home we love and desire before even making it a possibility. But then there's another option...

In the middle are open hands, cupped together like a bowl. "Lord, give what you want to give and take what you want to take." This is where we let God influence and take part in our home. We may have an idea of what we wanted it to be, and it's beautiful to honor ourselves. It is also important to keep our hands open and be flexible enough to let God be God.

This feels like freedom. This feels light and easy. This is trusting God to give and take, and also trusting ourselves to handle it well. This may mean getting more than we ever imagined—our dream home, a space that really feels like us! This may mean giving up something we really wanted for our home or having to wait and not get it now. Amazingly enough, friend, that feels really good too. It feels good to be unattached enough to trust and enjoy, no matter what. This feels like coming home.

Time and Energy

I'll touch briefly on the resources of time and energy. We chose to remodel when our kids were 6 and 4, with a baby on the way. We knew that once our baby was born, we would prefer not to carve out the time to invest in our home for probably a couple of years, and we wanted to be able to enjoy the remodel for as long as possible. For some reason, even while being sick and maybe physically tired, I tend to get a good ambitious energy during pregnancy, so that was a fit for me. We also knew from having two children how precious that first year of life is—albeit busy, but also irreplaceable.

We chose this time in life so that we could bring our little one back to a place that felt like home and then shift our focus toward this baby instead of toward the house. For me personally, at 37 years old, this was the first time in my life when I was willing to truly put in the time and energy to make our home a priority. Up until this point, while I occasionally bought an item or made an intentional decision about where we lived, and while I cared for our living space, it wasn't the focus. But in this season, I decided to go all in for our home. I started looking at design trends, flipping through home magazines, and keeping an eye out for those special items that just made my heart go pitter-patter.

Another aspect of time that I learned to honor is the value of letting things simmer. There were a few decisions in our home that really seemed right until they had time to just simmer in the background, allowing whatever questions or doubts to come out, and then seeing those answers through. For example, one frustration in our home was this 3-foot-wide hallway bottleneck with the coat closet. When we got home, whoever walked in first would open the coat closet door which blocked off the entire hallway, and the rest of us were trapped behind them while they were dropping off keys, putting shoes away, and removing outerwear, unable to access the closet or the rest of the house. This was already directly across from the door to the basement. Our first solution was to punch out the coat closet and replace it with a bench below the stairs for sitting and removing winter wear, with baskets underneath for shoes and gloves. However, after this process, I had a 3 AM epiphany that removing the coat closet was a downgrade for the whole house. Instead, we decided to still add the bench and change our habits so we gravitate there when we walk in instead of standing in the hallway. We also coat closet and basement doors to open the space so others can walk by. So we get to keep the coat closet and resolve the bottleneck with some creativity that would have never come without that simmering time.

Tip: One way to shorten the simmer time is to just ask yourself, "What do I want?" and, "Why do I want it?" Once you're satisfied with those two answers, how to get there gets easier and more fun too!

This is also why there's beauty in allowing the process to take the proper amount of time instead of rushing through it. When we moved into our home, we lived in it for about 6 months before renovating. Certainly, not every situation allows or needs that luxury, but if it's possible, there's an understanding of the natural flow of a home that is learned with that sweet time. There were items I would have changed had we started renovating immediately that I came to realize would come at a loss that I would not have even known about had we not let the home show us what it was before assuming we knew better.

If we'd remodeled right away, we would have removed the wall between the dining room and basement stairs to open up the floor plan more. As the months went by in our home, the kids would run down to the basement to play. Dave and I would get a little reprieve from the noise-level of excited, playing children since the basement was fairly closed off. We started to realize that if we tore out those walls, we would be destroying that quiet break as well. After 6 months in the home, the desire to remove those walls was gone completely. Then as we planned out the kitchen remodel, we ended up using that bare wall by the stairs to add cupboards for a pantry and a coffee bar. The storage space is invaluable and would not have been an option if we had hurriedly torn out that wall!

Kitchen Coffee Bar

My friend Mary Beth has created more than one beautiful home over the years, and she suggests patience for what we put on the walls. Leave the walls bare at first, and then if it still bothers you after a few months, add something. She said at first, she would hurriedly fill every wall, which led to feeling the need to hurriedly decorate around it. After years of creating beautiful homes, she learned to just let the space be. Often when each wall was decorated, it would make the space feel a little too busy.

The other aspect of time that isn't often talked about is the beauty of delayed gratification. In a world that hails instant gratification as the greater good, I'd like to give a little shoutout to its counterpart. Have you ever worked hard for something and eventually earned it yourself? The gratification feels so good. Have you ever decided to wait on something you want so that it could be a reward for some milestone or accomplishment? Or have you simply known a certain gift was coming and enjoyed the anticipation, which made it that much sweeter when it finally did come? All of these experiences feel so good. Often, with instant gratification, what also happens is almost instant dissatisfaction—shortly after getting whatever it was that was wanted, it loses its luster. Then we're left again feeling unsatisfied, looking for the next dopamine hit from the newest passing desire. So how does this relate to making a house a home, especially here in this resources section? Well, all that to say, sometimes the temptation to blow the budget and get that home, that remodel, or that latest piece of furniture/decor you want can be pretty strong. Let's use this awareness of the beauty of delayed gratification to build perspective and temper the temptation. It will be far more homey, comforting, peaceful, and enjoyable to be in your space knowing that what you did was done with self-control rather than out of impulse and a need for instant gratification.

How good does it feel to look around, even sitting on that couch that was bought for a good deal second-hand, knowing that you put this space together just right for where you are in life right now? In my first home, there was a black and white sketch of the Eiffel Tower that I'd bought for a few dollars from a street vendor in Paris while I was backpacking through Europe during summer vacation. Then I went to a discount store and found a beautiful black frame with a white mat. The artwork in the frame was a floral bouquet that didn't appeal to me at all, but that didn't matter. When I got home, I took apart the back of the artwork, removed the floral bouquet art, put in my inexpensive sketch from Paris, and for less than $20, had a beautifully framed piece of artwork with a great story behind it. That was satisfying. There's no replacement for taking a little step back and looking at a space with fresh eyes and a little creativity.

Even while we're joyfully anticipating what we hope our home to eventually be, we can learn to entirely embrace what it is right now and start having fun with it. For example, when Dave got his much awaited 10x20 shed/shop built, it came completely unfinished on the inside. The rafters were open, the joists were exposed, and the floor was bare wood particle board. Cole and Amora, ages 7 and 5 at the time, dragged in a couple of soccer goals and a ball and immediately took over the shop, making it their own little dream indoor mini soccer field. They then proceeded to try to convince Dave that this was the highest and best use of the shed and that he should donate his brand new, long-awaited building to the cause. One delightful memory is the whole family out in that bare little shed in the pouring rain having an intense and funny indoor soccer match. We joked that we would have to live out in this little field because the lightning storm was so strong, and the kids were delighted at the prospect of moving into that 200 square foot space all together as a family. Even now, writing this, I smile at the memory of how we enjoyed that space in the in-between.

Now, Dave has finished off the interior as his extra storage and a small shop. He ran electrical from the house out to the shed, buried the lines underground, put in a subpanel, ran wiring throughout, installed flooring, had it drywalled and painted, installed baseboards, put in light fixtures, outlets, and switches, and got a workbench. He's brought in the tools and items that he intended for that shed when it was first built. It looks and feels completely different. It's nice there now. And in a special way, it was nice in there too with the pouring rain and lightning outside, kicking around a soccer ball with those amazing little kids. If I could have, I wouldn't trade those memories of the unfinished part to have finished it sooner. No way.

Being Guided by the Rhythm of Life

There is something meaningful about allowing the rhythm of life to guide the sweet changes to our home. We had plans of putting in 2 floating wood shelves in the arched ledges on either side of the fireplace, and somehow, we hadn't gotten to it. I think there was also a subtle, small feeling holding us back, and so often that little whisper guides our life to where it should be if we let it. We could have gotten into a spiral of pushing ourselves to "just get it done," and if we had, the nativity set from Bethlehem that fell into our laps this Christmas wouldn't have fit either. It fits perfectly. It's amazing how our home, in small everyday ways, can teach us to let go of our own timelines and expectations to give space for God to do what He does.

Our daughter loves climbing up into the arch on the other side and playing with her critter dollhouse. If we added the shelves now, what we would gain in aesthetics for the grownups to enjoy would be outweighed by what we would lose in that bouncy little blonde girl crawling up into that special spot with her friend and imagining the day away. One day sooner than we think, that will have lost its appeal, and the beautiful wood ledge will probably take its place. I enjoy this precious season and also wait in joyful hope for the next one.

Key Takeaways

- Establishing a budget is foundational for creating a peaceful and joyful home environment; financial stress undermines the sense of "home."

- It's important to understand your current financial situation, including current balances, upcoming income, and expected expenses, to plan effectively.

- Distinguish between maintenance and upgrades, and remember that simple, budget-friendly changes can have a significant impact on how your home feels. You can make it a game to win with money when it comes to your home!

- Feel free to give yourself enough time to figure out the flow of your home, and work on your home in the ways that fit organically with your time, energy, and money.

Chapter 5

All that You Need and Nothing You Don't

Part of the definition of simplicity is "freedom from complexity." Isn't that the truth? When a room gets too full or too busy, it does feel stifling and oppressive. But remove some of the items and the freedom, openness, and simplicity returns. The organization gives us this gift too. It's freeing to know where to find something. It's liberating to know that we have the items in our home to thrive and aren't burdened by lots of unnecessary extras. Achieving this simplicity comes with a little intentionality.

Intentionality

There was a time when I falsely assumed that if I wanted to renew a space, the first step was to go shopping. Yet sometimes the fastest way to renew a space is to take items out, not bring more in. If a space has become cluttered, adding that special something to the room will just make it more overwhelming. Shopping can come with an innate, albeit short-lived, little high, but it doesn't make our space feel more like home unless it's done with intentionality.

Another alternative is to go shopping in your own home! Sometimes simply moving a few pieces around or pulling some small pretty items out of cupboards makes a bigger difference than we may realize. Recently, I added 2 small items to the center of the dining table. One is a white plate from Poland with beautiful, hand-painted blue flowers that I decided to use as a napkin holder. The other is a saki shot glass that's clear on top and blue glass on the bottom – I broke off a piece of greenery in a pot nearby and put it in the shot glass with a little water. Both little pieces were in cupboards, and both of them have meaningful family stories behind them. It heightened the class of the dining room and the personalization. No store-bought piece could have been quite as meaningful or personal. (Feel free to hop up and make little changes anytime you feel inspired. It can be fun, productive, and spontaneous. It usually just takes a few minutes. And it's free!)

We've done this in bigger ways too by changing the purpose of different spaces as we live in them and discover how our home fits with our family. What a beautiful process. When we reinvented the memories we wanted to make in each room, we'd move the furnishings around to fit the vision and eliminate clutter.

Clutter

With the level of abundance that we have in general in America today, so many of us are struggling with a problem of excess. I grew up in a home that epitomized this, as my mother had grown up in communist Poland and in an environment similar to America during the Great Depression. There are two primary roots of clutter. The first comes from a mindset of scarcity, which is rooted in fear that we won't have enough. This is certainly what people experienced during the Great Depression and what my mom experienced. That fear of scarcity causes us to cling to more than we need.

Another cause is actually rooted in indecision. We want to have lots of options available to us, so we stockpile more than we need in order to have every possible option available. Unfortunately, when we don't choose a lane or make decisions that commit to a certain path in life, rather than having the freedom to pursue everything, we actually rob ourselves of what we could have if we had been willing to commit. How this relates to our home and clutter is that perhaps we don't choose a direction for a room; instead, we just gather things in it that make "anything" work in that room. The irony is that in an effort to make everything work in that room, it seems that nothing works since it just becomes overwhelmed with stuff. This may be a living room that has the standard living furniture, overflowing toys, comfy beanbags, a desk that doesn't quite fit, and an oversized TV. We're trying to make one living space into a theater room, a playroom, an office, and a living room. Instead, we simply create a space that is unpleasant to be in and doesn't serve any of those functions well.

Again, the solution begins between our ears. First, take a step back and figure out what purpose or purposes for that room you're willing to let go of or at least make secondary. That may mean that this living room doesn't have a full office setup, but instead, there's a tray on the couch that you can put your laptop on when you want to work in the living room. This means that the living room invites you to relax and enjoy the space, but when the need arises to work, it still allows for it in a relaxing way.

The fast-paced culture we live in is another thing that hinders us from creating a home that is appropriately filled and feels good to be in. Items easily accumulate, such as party favors from a birthday, school supplies, paperwork, impulsive purchases, and whatever else we may bring into our home as we search for joy. All of these eventually clutter our space.

If this clutter crisis resonates with you at all, my offer to you is that the next time you have the resources of time and money to search for that next item to buy, instead use that precious time to think about your home and see what can be cleared out. This may even have the added benefit of increasing the monetary resources you have available, since you may be able to sell some of those excess items. If the items are not of the quality that can be sold, you may use the money that would have gone toward more items to instead pay to have things removed (or even better, you can save that money up!).

Marie Kondo's approach is so relevant here. Her primary suggestion is to look at an item and ask if it brings you joy. If the answer is no, you thank the item for having served its purpose in your life and get it out of your home. What a freeing experience!

A habit we have created is that before we buy an item that is going to come into our home, we first ask the question of where this will belong. This has been so helpful since if we do not have a good place to put something, then we don't have space for it in our lives or our home. This has helped me be a more discerning purchaser, and since the decision of where it will go has to be made anyway when you get home, this simply moves that decision slightly sooner so that we live with more intentionality. For example, if the only space for that new soccer goal is in the middle of the living room, it sure makes it easier to skip the purchase! It also helps me think through how this item would function in our lives. Will this be something we grab as we walk out the door? Is this an item I would use in the kitchen? Where does this fit? Sometimes, as I ask that question, it validates the purchase since I see more clearly where it would belong and add value to us. Other times, as I hinted at earlier, I see that in fact it would not improve the quality of our lives or our home.

Often, when we think of creating a home or improving our living space, we tend to jump to buying more items. If we already have more in our space than there should be, that would only perpetuate the problem and move us further from the home that we long for. Again, this work is free or nearly free! While we may find ourselves investing in some good storage solutions or paying a junk removal company, I have found that more often, we end up making a profit at a garage sale, getting the joy of donating items that other people can use, or taking a simple trip to the trash can if an item has exceeded its useful life.

To simplify, start by identifying how many items you have that serve the same purpose, and then decide which to keep. This is a simple exercise with broad application. For example:

- Are there three bottles of body wash and four different shampoos on the ledge in the shower? For items that get used up like shampoo, consider putting them away in an organized place so that you pull out the refills as needed.

- In my house growing up, we had a large TV stand, but when we upgraded to a TV too big for the stand, we simply placed a new table in front of the TV stand with the second TV. Consider listing these items for sale or for free to improve your home and someone else's.

- How many bowls in the kitchen serve the same purpose, and how many will you realistically use at one time? Consider giving yourself a timeline like a year, and if an item hasn't been used by then, pass it along. For kitchen items, a year works well since we may have belongings that are needed for holidays. Those items we can move to the harder to reach spaces, like the back of the cabinet or the top shelf, so we don't have to move them to get to our daily use items.

One of the great aspects of this kind of exercise is that it doesn't have to be done all at once. You can pick one room to start in or simply keep your eyes open for redundancies as you go about your home and day. As you find them, clear out the ones you like the least.

There is great peace and a release of tension that comes from letting go. This feels like freedom. This kind of loss is like losing the 10 pounds you've been wanting to get rid of for a while. It's exciting, exhilarating, and feels accomplished.

Redefining Waste

It takes courage to let go. It takes trust to get rid of an item that may be useful, that has a purpose, but that doesn't belong in your or my home. We have to trust that God will provide for us, that we will have what we need even if we let this go.

I put an unopened light fixture in a giveaway box. There was a time when I wouldn't have been able to do that, but we had bought it for a purpose that didn't work out, and it had sat in storage for a year. Perhaps it will end up in the perfect place, just not in our home.

Letting go opens up our spaces and opens the door to generosity, giving us the opportunity to bless others with things we no longer need. I've come to realize that cluttering up our home with items I'm not using, that someone else could use, is twice as wasteful. In the movie *The Grinch*, as Jim Carrey is digging through the dump, he makes the comment, "Well, you know what they say: One man's toxic waste is another man's potpourri!" Let's share our blessings, declutter our homes, and experience the freedom of living unattached.

Excess

Excess is not the same as abundance. When we pack our time excessively, we leave inadequate space for thinking, resting, being creative, laying under a tree, or connecting with those we love. When we hold onto more than we need, living in clutter and excess, we also rob ourselves of the joy, simplicity and fulfillment our homes can bring.

A picture is worth a thousand words, so here is a visual exercise to help make the point.

This is an AI generated picture of a living room that is minimal, simple, and uncluttered. Breathe it in. Notice it feels comfortable and still has a couple books by the couch, a mug on the coffee table, shades to draw if the sun gets too intense or for an afternoon nap on the couch, and plants.

This next image is similar since it still has the big window, curtains and couch. There's more stimulation with the extra color, which can be invigorating when it's not overdone, but here there are many colors. The couch has more pillows which make it a bit crowded, less relaxing and less inviting.

Instead of a couple books, there is a shelf that is pretty full. The window sill has stacked items, and the coffee table doesn't have enough space available for a snack plate or drink. The beauty and functionality suffer from the excess. How does this room feel to you? Can you imagine pulling items out of this room that would make it feel better, relaxing, right, balanced, and like it's serving you? Take maybe 30 seconds to a minute to imagine fixing this room.

This is another example with some clutter of a beautiful room. Here the colors are subdued so the color itself isn't overstimulating, but items are out of place, and there are a lot of items for the size of the space. I also notice the live plants are missing, so to me this is a room where more items would come out and a little greenery would come in. Clearing the loaded window sill and adding soft curtains would also balance this room so that it's more inviting and calming, less harsh and overwhelming. This room would also benefit from a 10-minute tidy up, folding the blanket on the couch, arranging the pillows, stacking the books, and clearing out or putting away items on the floor. For example:

The purpose of this exercise is to also show how these are beautifully renovated, yet the feeling of home is lost when excess comes in. It is worth protecting that space of having enough and not too much. It does take time and energy to sell, post, or giveaway items, to sort and donate. Hopefully seeing these pictures helps demonstrate the incredible value that comes from doing that work! Getting a bigger house doesn't solve the problem since the habit of decluttering will soon become necessary even there.

This is a skill, and you can learn it. You can hone it in and improve it. I have watched a beautiful, personalized, functional home lose that comfortable feeling by getting overfilled, and I have also personally witnessed that balance being restored when they moved a couple items back out. They put in the work, and it paid off daily for them! So it can be for you.

Before we finish this little exercise, let's look back at the first picture that feels like "aaah."

Hopefully going through this, by looking at someone else's space, has been helpful to you in being able to see the principles that you can use in your own home. How will you apply them? Take a deep breath, smile, and when you're ready, look at your own home. Use this same instinct that goes with your gut to see what is the excess and what needs to go, what is sucking the joy out of the room, and get it on out of there!

Exercise

What items or space comes to mind to declutter as you read this? _______

____

____

What item(s) are you holding tightly that are not actually making you feel abundant or at home? _______________________________________

____

This is the work of decluttering.

Tip: Often when we purge or minimize, it is tempting to hold on to at least 10-20% more than we should. We can base what we keep on the amount of space, even if that means we can barely squeeze the items in, more than basing it on what we truly need to thrive. Simply having the awareness that this is a common temptation can help you combat it.

Now celebrate your wins! Even if it was 1 or 2 items that cleared out, you just learned a skill. This is the beginning, or the continuation, of honing this skill. Go you!

Storage Units

Tip: There is a time and a place for a storage unit. Too often, a storage unit is used to store lots of items we have no reason to keep that we don't need, we don't use, and we probably don't even want. That's why we took them out of our home and put them in a storage unit. However, probably because of some scarcity belief, we hang on to it out of fear. That's not what I'm talking about here.

I'm going to show you the right way to use a storage unit and how to know if you should have one. Let's start with a story.

My amazing friend Cecilia lives in a pretty small home with her husband and four kids. Her husband has a job that requires a fair amount of equipment, and they homeschool their kids. The problem that can arise in that situation is clutter, which doesn't feel good. They do have some storage, but even with the space being well-managed, they've run out of room to store items under beds and in closets. This is why storage units exist.

They are able to store holiday decorations, seasonal items like winter clothes, camping supplies, items for hobbies that only need to be accessed when they're preparing for those activities, childhood sentimental items to pass on one day, and luggage nearby without cluttering up their home. They also use the storage for toy cycling, where they rotate toys so kids can get a break from them, not be overwhelmed by them, and rediscover them without having to buy new ones. In their situation with four kids, they can store clothing that will be reused but is between the current kids' sizes.

The cost of the storage unit is probably 10-15% of the cost of a bigger mortgage and a bigger home. By utilizing that external space, they're able to help their home feel big enough again without having all the hassle of a move or the expense of an upgrade. For them, a bigger house would come with too many sacrifices to be worthwhile. With the extra costs, this would require cutting out activities for the kids and giving up their fun money. We want our home to serve us, and when we go outside of our price range, that can easily flip so that we're working for our home instead. The storage unit can bridge that gap and bring order and space back into a home.

Some of their items, of course, won't apply to you. A good question to ask is, "How often will I use this item?" Then make a rule of thumb for what goes in the storage unit based on how often you plan to access it. For example, you may say anything we most likely won't use for a month or three months goes into storage. Now you have a system!

What to Keep and What to Let Go

There's an intentionality in letting go of the items that may be cluttering the space or that may have served their purpose. We find knick knacks and new items coming into our home almost constantly, so if there aren't other items going out the door, our home quickly becomes overfilled. We've become more discerning about what comes in and also accepted an almost revolving door idea of taking things out that have become worn out, outgrown, or that may serve someone else better than us.

Seasons in life present us with different needs and wants, children grow, and hobbies are allowed to shift. That's okay, in fact, it's beautiful. And with it sometimes comes bringing new items in, sometimes comes seeing old items in a new light, and sometimes means letting go.

So how do you know when to let go and when to hold on?

My friend Mary Beth offers a helpful perspective here as well. She said, "There are only a few things in the house that I really care about. I'll keep my parents' bedroom set forever. It was the first furniture they owned. They paid $75 for it. That and the hutch desk. That's it. The rest of it I could get rid of and wouldn't miss it!" This was the inspiration for my idea about how to know what to keep and what to let go. Start with a list of what items in your home are truly meaningful to you. My suspicion is that like Mary Beth, when we take a step back (and aren't looking around the room at each item), it's probably a pretty short list. My list is also a handful of items: our American-made comfy couch full of memories, the hand-carved artwork by Jason Waldron of the woman reaching up towards God, and the picture of my great, great grandfather in a vintage gold frame.

Exercise

What are the meaningful pieces for you in your home? _______________

____

____

____

Somehow, having a list of what means the most to me brings peace and order. It helps me let go of the rest of the items—not necessarily that they're all going out the door, because there are items in our home we use daily and enjoy, but somehow the pressure is off. If, in an attempt to declutter, we get rid of a little too much and later miss an item that would have still been useful, it's not as big of a deal. That gives me the freedom and space to declutter, even if I don't do it perfectly. As long as those listed treasures stay, the rest is replaceable; and for the greater perspective, to step back even further, we can't take it with us when we exit stage left. From dust we came, and to dust we will return.

Tip: If you think it will serve you, try pausing new home purchases for 40 days. This restful break can give fresh eyes for what's in your home and create space for creative rearranging and simplifying.

When in doubt, it may be best to return to the basics. Let's do that now.

The Essentials List

One of the reasons that a vacation getaway can be such a recharge is because it gives us fresh eyes. Staying at the "Millionaire Quartet" vacation rental in Saint George, Utah did that for us because all of the essential items were there without the clutter or excess. There was an organization. The decor was intentional. It rooted me back to the purpose of decor, which is to create a certain feel, an ambience, a personality to a home.

I've made this list extremely fundamental, and that's done on purpose. Staying in that vacation home helped me see what the essentials are, because I think often we live in excess from a place of not being sure if those items are necessary or not. If we aren't sure that we've covered the essentials, it makes sense that we would continue to acquire, or at least hold on to everything we've got. This is here to bring freedom and clarity. Seeing how nice it was to have the basics covered without the excess was inspiring, so I share it with you.

Also, this is formatted as a checklist with space for you to check off each item as you go through them. If there are any that don't apply for you, or if you have a few to add, feel free to make it your own.

Here is the essentials list by room.

Bathroom:
☐ Privacy. Door and lock.
☐ Toilet.
☐ Sink and faucet.
☐ Mirror.
☐ Light switch and switch for vent fan.
☐ Light and vent fan.
☐ Toilet paper holder.
☐ Toilet Scrub brush.
☐ Plunger.
☐ Toilet paper with refills available.
☐ Hand soap with dispenser.
☐ Lotion.
☐ Facial tissue holder.
☐ Facial tissue.

☐ Trash Can and trash bag.

☐ Towel holder.

☐ Towels.

☐ Outlet.

☐ Decor.

☐ Hook.

☐ Bath and/or shower.

☐ Shampoo, conditioner and body wash.

Entry:

☐ Decor (mirrors, picture, metal work).

☐ Doormat.

☐ Coat/purse hook or coat closet.

☐ Place for shoes (basket, rack, ledge under table or bench).

☐ Tabletop or bowl for keys and wallet.

☐ Optional: bench for sitting to put shoes on and take shoes off.

☐ Light switch and outlets.

Bedroom:

☐ Bed.

☐ Bed frame.

☐ Sheets, blankets, pillows.

☐ Preferable: Comforter and throw pillows.

☐ Bedside table(s) and lamp(s).

☐ Lighting, light switch.

☐ Closet/Storage.

☐ Preferable: fan.

☐ Rug or carpet.

☐ Dresser.

☐ Wall outlets.

☐ Mirror.

Dining room:
☐ Table and chairs.
☐ Light and switch.
☐ Wall outlet.
☐ Optional: hutch.

Living room:
☐ Light and switch.
☐ Couch.
☐ Couch pillows.
☐ Coffee table and side table(s).
☐ Blanket.
☐ Rug.
☐ Optional: fan and lamp.
☐ Optional: TV.
☐ Optional: TV console.
☐ Optional: Place for remote controls.
☐ Optional: basket, console, or ottoman storage for games.

Kitchen:
☐ Lighting and light switch.
☐ Vent fan.
☐ Sink, disposal and faucet. Sink stopper.
☐ Stovetop.
☐ Oven.
☐ Refrigerator.
☐ Countertop, drawers and cabinets.
☐ Outlets.
☐ Trash can and trash bags.
☐ Hand soap, lotion, dish soap, sponge, scrubber, dish cloths, dish towels, dishwasher soap and drying rack or drying towel.

☐ Paper towel holder and paper towels.

☐ Stockpot, 4 quart pot, and 2 quart pot

☐ Small, medium and large skillet pans.

☐ Steak knives, paring knife, bread knife, chef knife, and kitchen scissors.

☐ 2 Cutting boards.

☐ Spatula, spoons, pasta spoon, ladle, potato masher, Corkscrew, bottle opener, can opener, ice cream scoop, pizza slicer, peeler, and whisk.

☐ Barbecue tools and lighter.

☐ Small casserole dish with lid and large casserole dish.

☐ Set of three glass bowls with lids, three plastic mixing bowls, and colander.

☐ Plastic wrap, aluminum foil, and plastic zip bags.

☐ Mixer, measuring cups, measuring spoons, liquid measuring cup, and rubber spatula.

☐ Two serving bowls, two platters and a pitcher.

☐ Dinner plates, salad plates, and bowls.

☐ Plastic plates, plastic cups, and plastic bowls.

☐ Mugs, large glasses, small glasses, optional tiny glasses, optional ramekins.

☐ Tupperware.

☐ Silverware, 2 serving spoons and 2 serving forks.

☐ Cake pan, 2 cookie sheets, muffin pan, pizza pan and hot pads.

☐ Small appliances: coffee pot, blender, toaster, and griddle.

☐ Preferable: Dishwasher.

☐ Preferable: Backsplash.

☐ Optional: island and barstools.

☐ Optional: kids plates, kids bowls, kid cups, and kids plastic silverware.

The reason I put in such a comprehensive list, complete with the light switches and all, is because it helps us come back to the basics: what are the basics of a home? Identify them so we can hit those even with very simple items, and then we're covered. We can expand from there, and we have the option to upgrade, but we've covered the essentials. The rest is just gravy.

Remember, this list is here to serve and guide you, not to dictate. If your home is a 100 year old craftsman for example, or if you never cook pizza, your list will vary. Probably each of ours will be a little personalized. Still, having this list as a basic foundation creates a good launch point.

Waiting or Weeding

Waiting. When we finished the bulk of the remodel, I was tempted to fill our home with new furnishings, new decor, and the latest trendy items I had been seeing in pictures and magazines while we were planning, researching, and making remodel decisions. Thank God that didn't happen. When our baby was born, we hit the pause button on home projects. This has ended up being a tremendous blessing. So spaces stayed open and some walls remained bare for a few months. Then slowly and organically, the right piece for the right space started to reveal itself. Something beautiful happened: a natural blending of the old and new that became far more interesting, personalized, and meaningful than the latest all-new pieces could have ever been.

Weeding. As my friend Dori Day, a woman who truly understands the meaning of home, says, "Weeding is way harder." At first, I wasn't sure what she meant by that comment, but then she went on. After she and her husband built their dream home, she had this gnawing, almost desperate need to fill the walls and have stuff up, for the home to feel 'done.' So they hurriedly ordered items, found items, and asked friends to make items that they thought they would like, and in short order, every wall had something on it. Then they stepped back. The home was not satisfying. It did not feel right. "I would sit in a room, and I couldn't figure out why I didn't like it. Was it the artwork on the wall? Was it something else? I didn't know what was the harvest and what were the weeds, what should be kept and what should be pulled. I didn't know what to take out and what to leave, but I knew it didn't work, I didn't like it, and it didn't feel like my home. Weeding is way harder than waiting." Over the course of a few weeks, they did purge, and weed, figure it out and make it home. The list of basics and of your meaningful pieces sure helps too.

When we started putting up old little pieces in new combinations and ways, the stories behind them came alive. The first collage I put on a wall was emotionally overwhelming in the most enjoyable way: a 250-year-old picture of my great-great-grandfather, who was a general in the Polish Army; a simple round mirror that had hung on my wall in Florida before my husband and I even met; a white-framed angel from Italy given to us as a gift when our oldest son was born; a cross with the risen Lord; and an antique picture of a young child my mother gave me that looks much like a combination of all our children smooshed together.

Old and new treasures

So we let go of some items that don't bring us joy, treasure a select few others, and bring in some new ones. We hold them lightly. This is the mindset journey from scarcity to minimalism to abundance – an abundance that's organized, that includes those items that bring joy and that improve our quality of life in small ways without being cluttered or unnecessary. We both let go of some items and are willing to bring in others.

What We Allow Into Our Home

Remember the unseen. Over the years, I have found that some items rob our space of peace and seem to disrupt our minds. For example, there was a red dragon toy that scared one of the younger children. After two or three days with this toy in our house, we found ourselves bickering with each other and noticed the kids weren't sleeping as well. It would be easy to overlook that object as the cause if we weren't aware of the fact that this is possible. I think we more easily recognize that having Holy items in our space does the opposite. Having a cross and a Bible invites the Holy Spirit in and makes our home less desirable for those forces that aren't on that winning team. The cross also reminds us to look beyond ourselves, to look up, and to remember that in the realm of eternity, so much of what can get to us just doesn't matter.

On the other hand, some objects have the opposite effect. We threw that dragon toy in the trash, and then the peace returned to our home. We've had a few similar experiences with other objects or even lingering energies in a room like a spirit of restlessness that made us feel like we were never allowed to relax, even at night.

Develop an awareness of what energy an object, person, or emotion may bring into your home. Evict that which is not serving you and which is sucking the joy and peace out of the air. We prayed against the spirit of restlessness and invited the Holy Spirit to come in and fill that space. The feel of our home changed for the better. I slept better after that prayer. We both evicted the restlessness and then filled that space with God's presence and glory. Let this serve as an invitation to pay attention to the gut feelings that the Holy Spirit so graciously provides and to protect your home from that which does not give life to the fullest.

Creating a Home with Hotel Comforts

On a lighter note, there are certain staples at a hotel that make it feel like a novel experience, and there's no reason we can't have those in our own homes. What a great life hack, to make our daily living space a place that feels like a vacation and that we don't want to leave. A few of those touches can be a comfortable bathrobe, cozy slippers, a bowl full of mints, toothpicks if you like them to bring a restaurant vibe, a coffee bar, and comfortable bedding. The unseen message of a bathrobe, to me, is warmth, comfort, and relaxation. What homey invitations to add to our everyday living spaces. Live the best life that you can, and make yourself at home!

Key Takeaways

- Creating simplicity and decluttering your home can bring a sense of freedom and allow you to share excess items with others who need them.

- Use an "essentials list" to guide you in determining which items are truly necessary for you to thrive in your home, and let go of items that are not on the list.

- Adopting the "Marie Kondo" approach of asking if an item brings you joy can be helpful in the decluttering process; if it doesn't, consider getting rid of it.

- Balance introducing new items with appreciating and repurposing older ones to create a more personalized and meaningful home.

Chapter 6

Tiny Powerhouse Routines

In this chapter, we'll explore some small but mighty routines that simplify home care, balance expectations, and help you build lasting habits that make daily life easier. As human beings, we are creatures of habit. James Clear says, "You don't rise to the level of your goals—you fall to the level of your systems." Routines are not meant as rigid rules but rather as gentle anchors—predictable patterns that reduce mental load, bring clarity, and make the daily work of home more manageable.

Small Habits with Big Impact

There are some areas of a room that typically draw our attention first, and these are often the big, flat spaces in the middle of the room. Making the bed, clearing or tidying the coffee table, tidying the kitchen island, and clearing the dining table are big bang for buck items. Even if we just took care of those items, it would be a pretty nice power clean! In the bathroom, closing the shower curtain, straightening the mat, and placing the soap neatly can be done quickly. Clearing the countertop is quick too after we take the time once to designate spots in drawers or containers for toothbrushes and bathroom items that end up on the counter). Then, every time I walk past the bathroom, in a subtle way, I like our home and feel on top of it. Isn't that worth the few minutes of time?

Tip: Notice angles. For example, in the baby's nursery, I like the back of the rocking chair to line up with the wall behind it. It's small and so simple to do. Making that tiny change makes the whole room look just right.

Avoiding the Trap of Perfectionism

As a gentle reminder, while a clean, tidy home feels safe and welcoming, it's easy to cross the line into being ruled by perfection. A spotless house doesn't necessarily create a home. We can probably agree that a place smelling like dirty socks with the threat of a cockroach is not cozy—but there is a healthy middle ground.

Every family has different comfort levels. In our house, my husband prefers things quite tidy, and I honor that because it helps him feel at peace. But if I slip into a tense, pressured mindset—cleaning to make him happy—no one enjoys being home. He notices my tension and starts cleaning to make *me* happy, and suddenly we're both working hard but no one is relaxed.

When I pause and remember that love, joy, and connection matter more than the chores, everything shifts. A home is made up of the people in it, not the perfection of the space. When we keep that truth at the center, everyone can breathe and be themselves.

The Power Clean

When I'm trying to figure out what to prioritize in a room, I'll stand back and look at the entire space. Usually there are a few items that stand out first, so I'll go pick up those or clean that mess. Then I'll stand back and look at the entire room again. Now with those first few items addressed, usually something else catches my eye as being out of place or dirty, so I prioritize those next. This simple system can be so helpful, because it helps us get out of the details and see the bigger picture. I'm listing this first for the power clean because it's a universal principle that works from the living room to the lawn. Once I've done this a few times in the same room, it becomes pretty quick. This is how to train your eye to see what will have the biggest impact. This may add a minute or two in the beginning, but it is well worth it in the time it saves long term. Now I can usually get a glance of the living room and power clean in less than five minutes because it's usually the same toys that are out and I already know where they belong. But this is the first trick that helped me get there.

Tidying Tips

As I move about the house, my hands are rarely empty. When I see an item out of place and am headed into the other room, I've trained myself to bring items with me so they end up back where they belong. We put items at the bottom of the stairs that need to go upstairs and vice versa. Then when I head up, I usually take the extra 60 seconds to put the few items away before doing what I went upstairs to do. If I can't spare the 30 seconds to 2 minutes then, I'll simply place the items at the top of the stairs which only adds a few seconds of time. For me, this feels good since it's efficient and I like getting things done. I don't feel like I have to do it but rather prefer this method. The dining table is an area that gets dumped on quickly and is a visible space that I like to have cleared, so that's a good place to start with clearing out. I'll move dishes to the sink or dishwasher, hang up backpacks and coats, sort mail, and move items that have piled at least to the right staircase.

This is my nerdy side coming out but forming "metrics" around daily household items has been empowering for me. For example, the bed is usually the centerpiece of the bedroom, so if it's made, the entire room looks better. It takes me one to three minutes in the morning, depending on how tousled the sheets got overnight, and it instantly creates a sense of order and calm. If I have five minutes available and know I can tidy up that bathroom in 2, I go for it instead of thinking there's not enough time. It was incredibly easy to build these "metrics"! Simply glance at the clock when you start unloading the dishes (or whatever task you'd like to measure) and then glance back when it's done. Metric complete! Isn't that fun?

Within a few weeks of starting this little game in my mind, I have an internal list in my head of how long it takes to do those routine tasks and am able to fit them in more naturally. Come to think of it, the tasks that are still a little intimidating to me, the ones that burn energy just getting myself hyped up to do them, are the ones I haven't done this with yet, like cleaning the bathroom or mopping. We can build metrics together.

The other nice aspect of having these metrics is that it helps us have grace for ourselves. For example, if we have 20 minutes available and have a general idea of the time it takes to complete the chores, we can pick which ones to complete and let go of the rest for the day instead of feeling guilty that we didn't scrub top to bottom. This helped me one day when I was going to do the 5-minute dishes but our young son Mark filled a diaper right before we left to pick up the kids from school. It was an intentional reprioritization to leave the dishes and clean the baby. Since I could see it in that light, I didn't feel guilty about the dishes.

Another little brain hack is that I've set a rough limit to how many times I will let myself go past a small item that needs to be done before I just do it. Every time that we notice it and realize that it needs to be done, it takes energy. Often that little task can be done in a minute or two, and then it clears up our mental space and makes it happy for us to walk through our home again. So, my casual limit is 2 to 3 times. Examples include a little dirt pile on the floor, the smudge on the kitchen counter, or the toy out of place in the middle of the room. Sometimes I take care of it right away, but if not, this kicks in as a reminder and helps me feel better in my own home. In fact, I'm going to clean that little smudge off the pillow now…

Tip: We're allowed to have different standards for different areas. For example, our front room is more tidy and decluttered than the basement playroom on most days.

The Option of Leverage

Is there a laundry service in your area where you can outsource that daily task to buy some of your time back? These often cost less than one might think. Outsourcing grocery shopping and meal planning to a company that delivers all that you need for a few meals a week, based on the size of your family, is another great way to leverage help and free up mental space.

Along the same lines, can housework be outsourced? The idea of paying someone to do our family chores was a difficult one for me to accept at first, and for us having children, I realized part of it was wanting to teach them skills, work ethic, and humility. The balance we've found is doing the vacuuming, mopping, and bathrooms once a month as a family. Then two weeks later, we outsource those same cleaning tasks. This keeps the kids grounded, teaches them valuable and applicable life skills, and teaches them to contribute to the family and the home as well. Then once a month, as long as we have the means financially, I am willing to outsource those chores to get back a Saturday.

My friend Lydia Black built a simple and sustainable home system that started with leveraging a meal service three times a week. She would pick out the next three weeks worth of meals, and then the groceries with recipes would be delivered once a week. Then she would fill the box that the food came in with items from her basement that she was trying to clear out. The time and mental space she had been using to grocery shop and menu plan went towards decluttering, and she even reused the box the food came in to do it. Fantastic!

Example of Cleaning Based on Seasons of Life

We lived in an apartment for a month while our home was being remodeled. At the time, I was pregnant and in the third trimester. The half day of moving was exhausting, and so my expectations for that temporary home adjusted to the season of life.

Three days after moving was the first time I had the energy to do some very simple tasks to make the space feel more like home. I made the bed and cleared off the coffee table. That's it. The six paper grocery bags full of pantry items were still sitting on the floor in the kitchen. The bathroom counters were all pretty unorganized. But I gave myself the grace to let those be, to wait, to give my body, mind, and growing baby the rest needed. Since I adjusted my expectations to the season of life, I was able to feel at home even before it was at my normal expectation level.

I could have wasted those tired days feeling guilty or overwhelmed, and feeling inadequate because of the mess. But that would have meant ignoring the unique season of life I was in. In this example, when a good bit of my energy is going toward growing a human being, of course, there is less energy for tidying up, and that's okay. There are many examples that work here to demonstrate adjusting reasonable expectations based on the season of life.

So there were two tidy spaces I could see, two spaces that are focal to the rooms they're in, where my eyes could rest and get some relief from the mess. Did I hope to organize more and tidy up the space better in the future? Yes, sure. But right then, with the energy available to me, I could feel at home by being satisfied and not letting this temporary situation mean anything about me.

Without the energy to do more physically, I decided we needed to start with the space between our ears. One evening, while the family was together, I brought up the conversation about how home is anywhere that we are together. For the first time since we got there, all of a sudden, the kids got excited to be there. Cole said the bedroom that we all share, with the kids' mattresses on the floor, was his favorite room here. Being six years old, he couldn't really explain why, but I wonder if it's because this is something special they rarely get to do at home: to share a room together as a family and have sleepovers every night. Then Amora, at four years old, said she wants to stay here forever. Even at such a young age, I think they get it. Home is much more than fixtures and paint colors. We've heard the phrase "Home is Where the Heart Is." This was my experience of that truth.

Catch Alls – what to do with the dreaded "maybe" piles

I'll share some examples of ideas that we've come up with over time to organize different parts of our home. Some of these will apply to you, and others won't, but each of them has value since they teach a way of thinking that can be reapplied to various situations once the concept is grasped.

Giveaway pile: We used to have a paper bag as a permanent fixture in our main floor closet because as soon as we filled it up with items we no longer wanted or needed, inevitably one more item would show up that no longer belonged. Finally, I made the connection that what I thought was a temporary giveaway bag is more of a revolving door. Now we have a large, dedicated bottom drawer in the kitchen just for giveaway items. I'll sometimes also use it for borrowed items that need to be returned or items that someone left with us accidentally, like our own lost and found. When the drawer is full, that's the cue to move those items along.

Kids' clothing: Clothes that are still too big, or that the kids have outgrown, also used to be items that didn't have a place. Now, we have two canvas boxes in one of the kids' closets. One box is for clothing that is the next size up for our youngest, and the other box is for clothing that any of the kids have outgrown. Instead of dealing with those items one at a time, or having them set out until I get to it, they have this intentional spot. When the box is full, then it's time to sort it into the giveaway pile or into the storage bins of clothes that another child will grow into later (this could also work if I'm between sizes and have my own clothes that will fit again later).

Tip: This same concept works for seasonal clothes, maternity clothes, and different sizes. For example, If I'm working towards my ideal weight and am between sizes, move those items that don't fit into bins temporarily, or sort all those hangers to one side, so we're not flipping through them everyday if they're not in use right now.

Mail: Nowadays, we usually try to sort mail as soon as it gets here, but sometimes a piece of mail comes with a to-do item that takes a little more time. In our coat closet, we added a shelf that has key hooks and space for magazines or papers. This is where we put mail that requires a little more work. On my best days, I'll also add a note into my calendar or into the notes on my phone with a calendar reminder for when I plan to get to that mail.

Magazines: These used to sit on that dreaded kitchen counter spot for stuff to do. Now, if we want to read them later, I put them on the table next to the couch. This invites us to relax and enjoy the magazine instead of standing by the trash can reading it. If no one has made it a priority to read the magazine within a few weeks, we usually just toss it. This also helps us avoid reading a sales magazine of some sort just because it's there instead of being intentional with our time in our home.

Projects: This is a broader category, and I think it makes a good note to end this section on to solidify the thought process that applies to any catchalls. For extracurriculars and school projects, we have a small file in the cabinet by the dining table where the kids do their homework. Their current projects go into the paper file next to the pencils and school supplies, so they know where to find them. If we have a project we're working on that's 3D, I try to put it into a bin. We have shelves that hold bins on either side of the fireplace and can repurpose a bin for a project there. This idea of using a bin, drawer, or intentional spot that doesn't sit in the middle of the room can be used for a woodworking project, a honey-do project, a work project, etc. The overarching concept is that we don't want our home to feel like a 'to-do' list as we walk through it. Usually, we will get those projects done much sooner by putting them on the calendar or setting a reminder alarm to go off at a point in time when we will be able to address it. Then we can put it away out of sight and go back to enjoying our living space. Aaaah…

There's a powerful concept here: when we know where items belong and have routines for generally getting items back to those spots, the amount of work needed to get our home ready for guests or feeling good again goes down dramatically. Rarely does our main floor get messy enough that I can't do a basic tidy in ten minutes or less. This is what I want for you, if it's not already there, and it is completely attainable. A friend can call saying they're on the way over, and by the time they pull up ten minutes later, I can have those visual spots tidied and feel ready for them. Getting that basic organization, with the routines and habits to keep it going, is what creates that result.

Tip: When deciding where something will belong, try asking, "where would I look for this?"

Routines are life-giving because they give us simplicity and mental clarity that creates space in our homes, minds, and hearts. We don't have to think and rethink how to handle these repetitive tasks since we do that work once and then make a little system. Every time you do that, you get to leverage it over and over!

Key Takeaways

- Establishing these little powerhouse routines provides mental clarity and frees up time by automating repetitive tasks, making home maintenance more manageable.

- Prioritize "big bang for buck" tidying tasks that have the greatest visual impact, such as making the bed, clearing the coffee table, or tidying the kitchen island.

- Develop personal "metrics" for household tasks to better estimate time needed and fit them into your schedule more efficiently.

- Adjust your expectations for tidiness and cleanliness based on your current season of life, recognizing that your energy and priorities may shift.

- Create intentional spots for daily items like donations, kids' clothes, or mail to prevent clutter and keep your home feeling organized.

Chapter 7

Renovations and Remodels

"We shape our buildings; thereafter they shape us." - Winston Churchill. These words of Churchill ring true in our own renovation journey. When we undertake remodels and renovations, we're doing more than simply updating aesthetics or fixing structural issues. We're creating the backdrop for our daily stories, the stage for our memories, and an environment that either supports or hinders the way we want to live.

A renovation updates what's already there—refreshing, repairing, or improving the space without changing its basic layout. A remodel goes a step further by changing the structure, layout, or function of the room. Renovation makes it nicer; remodeling makes it different.

Imagine a typical family home that needs some changes. It has good bones, a lot of charm, but the kitchen feels cramped, and the flow between rooms just isn't right. For years, the folks navigate these quirks, adapting as best they can. But then comes the moment to renovate, to truly make the space their own. It isn't just about new countertops or fresh paint; it is about opening up the kitchen to become the heart of the home, where laughter and cooking intertwine. It is about creating a seamless flow that encourages togetherness, rather than isolation. The result wouldn't be just a remodeled house, it would be a space that truly feels like *home.*

In this chapter, we'll explore the many facets of renovations and remodels, going beyond surface-level improvements to focus on the deeper considerations that transform a house into a haven. Let's dive in and discover how thoughtful changes can dramatically enhance your daily life, creating a space that resonates with who you are and serves you.

Embedding Scripture in the Walls

Before painting or putting in new cabinets, when the room is stripped down to the studs, write scriptures into the walls. We went around the house with a pencil and did what no one will be able to see but that everyone will be able to feel. We wrote Bible verses on the drywall or onto whatever was going to be covered as we remodeled. God's Word has been embedded into our home.

Renovation Budget

An early consideration and foundational element is counting the cost, so that as you go through this, you have a good framework of how big a project this will be. Flip to Appendix B for your full Renovation Budget. This one includes all those items that are so often left out, leaving homeowners overspent and overtaxed. Fortunately that won't be you.

Tip: If you're just starting to think about what you want from your renovation or remodel, a good place to begin is with a list of priorities of what you want for your home. What do you dream of for your home? Enjoy…

When we first started renovating investment homes, our mentor John Burley told us, "Whatever budget you think it will cost, double it." My background was in finance, so I thought that wouldn't apply to me. Well, he was right! We planned on spending $3,000 on a small home to put in some very basic carpet, a little fresh paint, and a few other touch-ups. By the time we had taken care of those items and the ones that popped up along the way, we were right around $6,000! Even after decades of experience, John Burley adds a buffer to his budgets. He's able to hit his budget because he's already added in extra funds to account for unexpected costs.

Unless you're doing all the work yourself, typically the budget begins with a bid from a contractor, a store such as Home Depot, a designer, or several different contractors (cabinetry, countertops, plumbing, electrical, landscaping, etc.). So often, these bids don't include all the costs that the homeowner will incur. Some expenses that you may need to add to the bid to capture the full costs are:

1. Taxes, Shipping, and Fees

2. Materials not included in the bid: For example, our landscaping bid did not include the cost of pavers because those costs would be added after we selected the specific ones we wanted. Similarly, our design bid excluded smaller items such as table decorations, pillows, blankets, and comforters since these would be chosen in-store and charged based on actual costs once all other work was complete.

3. Any labor not included in the bid: For example, our interior design bid did not include the labor for the electrician to install the new light fixtures, for the carpenter to install wood beams, or for the wallpaper installation. Another example is when replacing bathroom or kitchen countertops, this typically does not include the cost of the plumber to install the faucet after the new countertop is in. Think through what will be needed for a complete and usable space, not just the next step.

4. Markups: Does the contractor or designer markup material costs to pay for their labor to get those supplies, and if so, is that cost included? This is normal, and I typically see it included. Sometimes

designers get wholesale pricing and pass those savings along to help offset the markups. Just find out.

5.   Holding costs: For example, if this is a major remodel, particularly if you won't be living there while all or some of the work is happening, what will you pay in electricity, gas, garbage pickup, lawn care, and other utilities while the work is being done? How much will you spend on the mortgage payments, and how much will you spend where you will be living during that time? Will you have extra food costs if you'll be eating out while the kitchen work is occurring? Will there be more gas in commuting or driving back and forth to the home to check on progress? A good place to start in estimating these costs is with your budget and then adding in the duplicate expenses such as rent where you'll stay in the meantime.

6.   Finance costs such as interest charges or credit card fees. This is $0 when paying cash.

7.   Maintenance and repairs: does the contractor guarantee their work? What happens if rework is needed? Will that be an extra expense? Or if something is damaged during the remodel, who pays for the repair? This isn't necessarily something to add at the beginning but further supports having extra cash in the bank and in the budget.

It is also a good rule of thumb to get three bids before hiring someone for the work. This may sound unnecessary, but we have found this to generally be worth the effort. Not only can there be a difference of thousands of dollars between their prices, but there can also be a wide range in their expertise. Oftentimes, talking to another contractor in the same trade and asking a few questions can teach us enough to see which ones actually know their stuff. This doesn't just save money but can also avoid huge headaches by hiring someone who does the work correctly. By the third conversation, you can usually tell which contractors are competent and which offer good value.

Once you have the bid you're planning to use, hold it up against the seven expenses listed above. Do you need to add in any of the expenses mentioned? Remember that the bid is typically just what you will pay the contractor. Make sure you've included any other costs to you so that you have the complete picture. Be a budgeting rock star!

Tip: Think through all the steps of your project from start to finish. If there are costs that aren't included yet, add them in.

Flow and Function Remodel Considerations

In our journey of transforming houses into homes through remodeling, we've encountered numerous functional aspects that significantly impact daily living. This section delves into a compilation of practical considerations that arose during our own renovation experiences, offering insights to optimize the flow and functionality of your space.

1. **Walkways** - The rule of thumb is 36" around each piece. For example, we measured out the dining room several times before deciding on what size dining table to get based on this rule of thumb. We included a little extra space to account for chairs that would be tucked into the table when they weren't in use but would still stick out a few inches past the table itself.

2. **Bottlenecks** - Consider how people move through your home. In ours, a narrow 3-foot hallway near the coat closet created a bottleneck. The first person entering would open the closet door and drop off belongings, blocking others from passing until they close the door. Initially, we thought about removing the closet, replacing it with a bench and baskets for shoes, plus hooks behind the front door for coats and bags. Later, I realized losing the closet reduced the home's functionality. So instead, we got the bench, removed the closet and basement doors, refinished the trim, and added hooks at both kid and adult heights along with a shelf for

keys and mail. This solution looks good, maintains function, and opens up the space.

Bottleneck Solutions

3. **Placement and Height of the Microwave** — Since hot items will be pulled out of the microwave, often full of liquid like in the case of soups, we were intentional about not putting the microwave too high in the kitchen. This was especially important since I stand at a whopping 5'2." This is relevant to other appliances as well, but for some reason the microwave seems to be the one that gets placed unusually high or low, almost like an afterthought, in kitchens we've seen.

4. **Clearance around the Refrigerator** — Since a refrigerator is often open with a person standing in front of it, we made sure to have extra clearance in this area. Our kitchen has an island so that a person can walk around the other side of the island and get past the refrigerator if it's in use. However, if this was not the layout and

there was only one way past the fridge, I would have allowed 4' or more around the fridge.

5. **Space in the Kitchen** – Our kitchen works best with 2 people cooking in it and is large enough to accommodate a couple helpers. If this would primarily be a space just 1 person was using, I would have put the sink, refrigerator, and stove closer together in a nice triangle.

6. **The Kitchen Triangle** – A good rule of thumb is to make sure the sink, the refrigerator, and the stove make a triangle between each other without anything (like an island) blocking the way. Notice how kitchens in cooking shows are set up this way. This helps with the flow.

7. **Measure Furniture and Fixtures** – A secret I learned from being around designers is measuring out and maybe even taping off spaces to show rugs and furnishings. For a bigger remodel, this can also be done for cabinets, appliances, etc. Measure furniture and fixtures so the size is appropriate for the space.

8. **Consider the Size of Light Fixtures** - When we moved into our home, the dining room chandelier was way too big for the space and overpowered the room. The result was that the entire room looked too small. A good rule of thumb for hanging light fixtures over a dining table is that the bottom of the fixture should be 30-36" above the top of the table.

9. **Items you Touch Every Day** – Think about doorknobs, faucets, handles, and any items you touch on a daily basis. What do they feel like in your hand? These are good places for pops of money. You get about 80% of the effect by just replacing the hardware on

a door as you do from an entirely new door in general (unless the door is a real standout piece).

Handles you touch often

10. **Comfort of Furniture Versus Aesthetics** – We bought our Milford couches with the upgraded cushions because we sank into them, like falling into a cloud and being enveloped in comfort. They're also beautiful, but they're even more comfortable. For an accent chair that's mainly aesthetic and won't probably be sat in to watch a movie, you may choose fashion over comfort. If it's a lounging spot that you think will get frequent use, consider both and perhaps put more emphasis on comfort.

11. **Kitchen Cabinets** – Before ordering cabinets, map out where you'll store key items. Knives, spatulas, and spices work well near the stove, for example. This gives you the opportunity to include a knife holding insert in a drawer and to get a pull out spice drawer in the right spot. Making this one-time effort ensures better flow

and makes daily tasks easier. Consider grouping related items together like serving dishes and ordering inserts or cabinetry made for cutting boards, for example. A little thoughtful planning now saves hassle and improves your kitchen's functionality for years.

12. **Deep Kitchen Drawers** – A very experienced, high end contractor suggested using deep, pull out drawers as often as possible in the kitchen instead of cabinets. What fantastic advice. Drawers make it easier to reach items towards the back without having to dig and move items in front of them. Drawers glide open. Deep drawers can hold substantial items like pots and pans or small appliances. Other than the places where we decided on smaller drawers specifically for knives, utensils, aluminum foil, and silverware, deep drawers work better since they are convenient and versatile.

Pull Out Drawers

13. **Highly Visible Areas** - What spaces do you want visible, and which are harder to keep tidy? The kitchen sink, for example, is part of the home that we didn't want front and center. Our original kitchen design had the sink on an island in the middle of the kitchen. But when we have guests over or are sitting down for dinner, that space

will be full of dirty dishes from the meal prep. It would have been visible from almost every spot on the main floor of the house, including the front door. Instead, we redesigned the kitchen to move the deep farmhouse sink to the back wall with a big window overlooking the backyard. We also added a shallow top cabinet to the left of the sink that we brought all the way down to the countertop so that it obstructs the view from the dining room for when the dishes get piled up. The parts of the kitchen that are easier to keep clean get the spotlight, and as an added bonus, we get a nice view into the outdoors while doing the dishes.

Cabinet makes dishes less noticeable

14. **The Little Kitchen Items** – I heard a designer comment on multiple clients she worked with who spared no expense on a kitchen remodel but then left an old rag on the counter and paper towels sitting out. That inspired me to get a simple mounted paper towel holder, a tray for the scrub brush and sponge, and a couple suction mounting hooks inside the sink for washcloths. The kitchen feels organized with a small investment of time and money. We also have a drying mat for handwashing dishes that I'll put on the

counter when it's in use and then tuck into the drawer once the dishes are dry and put away.

15. **The Direction the House Faces** – The South side of the home will get more sunlight and thus be warmer than the North side. In the summer, a friend was complaining that their house had South facing rooms that were unbearably hot, with the blinding sun shining in and the A/C unable to keep up. They ended up moving out! But there are solutions like adding a second A/C vent to those rooms, tinting those windows, and hanging blinds or curtains. Those also prevent the sun from discoloring and wearing out the furniture and flooring prematurely. An HVAC company can also install a fan in the attic to improve airflow and cool the home. In the winter, those will probably be the favorite rooms in the home as we search for sunshine and warmth. We considered moving the dining room into a front room of our home on the North side but ultimately kept it by the kitchen on the South side of the home so we could enjoy the sunshine.

16. **Outer Walls** – Consider temperature variations between walls that are on the outside parameter of the home compared to inner walls between rooms and in the interior of the home. My husband Dave pays attention to that detail and moved the baby's crib into an inner wall so that the temperature in the crib didn't fluctuate as much. If you're always too hot or too cold on the couch for example, is it on an outer wall? Can it be moved into the home away from the outside wall?

17. **Views from Windows** – We're used to prioritizing this if we're staying in an oceanfront hotel on vacation or if we live somewhere with stunning views, but what about the ordinary windows in our home? Our kitchen originally had 2 windows right next to each

other at the corner of the home. Looking out the right side window looked right at the side of the neighbors house. Looking out the left window, the view was of the very edge of our backyard, so if the kids were playing or we wanted to see the nicer part of the yard, you could barely see it by leaning forward and looking as far to the left as possible. We could have added blinds to distract from the view. We ended up moving the windows, sealing those off, and adding a bigger picture window that looked straight into the backyard where we could see the trees and the children play.

Tip: When working with contractors, especially for a bigger remodel, it's worth the effort to get three bids. The obvious benefit is potentially saving thousands of dollars. On a bigger remodel, we have seen the difference in price reach 6 fig

ures between different contractors! You'll also learn. We've gotten many ideas from contractors. We've also found that after talking to three people planning to do the same work, it's easier to get an idea of which one(s) actually know what they're doing. Imagine the headaches, rework, and problems that are avoided by working with someone competent!

Think about Your Home in Each Five-Year Season of Life

This is a simple, short exercise that can pay big dividends, especially while making bigger changes to a home. Take a few minutes to think about what life will be like five, ten, and twenty years from now. How old will the kids be if that's a consideration, what might you want and need later in life, and how might a room be repurposed in the future as hobbies and mobility change? There have been a few decisions we made based on this simple and dreamy exercise like getting the 5 year warranty on a new couch in a season with young kids and opting out of low shelves that would become a ladder up onto the counter for creative little ones. We also may prioritize durability if this is a season with pets or high wear.

Make a Space for Each Person to Love

Our kitchen remodel plan was starting to come together, but it didn't feel homey yet. It didn't feel like us yet. Then I started thinking about what would make the kitchen a space that Dave would love. My husband likes to start his day with a good cup of coffee. The part of the kitchen that is an ode to Dave is our little coffee bar area, complete with espresso machine, coffee grinder, double-walled glass mugs, and canisters of fresh coffee beans. This Dave station gets used often multiple times a day.

For the kids, we put a super Susan in one of the corners dedicated to them. One of the most popular items in their kids' corner has turned out to be the old toaster oven. It's nothing special to look at, but that 10-year-old appliance is a workhorse. We considered putting it in a giveaway box and then nonchalantly added it to the kids' corner instead. What a great repurpose that has turned out to be! I equate it to the Easy-Bake Oven. Our 7-year-old, Cole, is able to cook French fries and chicken nuggets fairly independently by putting it up on the counter and following the simple instructions I taught him. Yesterday, he made two batches of French fries for breakfast for the family. Personally, I would have cooked them a couple of minutes longer, but a plate of breakfast showed up in front of me, and I ate it happily. There are also bowls, measuring spoons, muffin cups, and a few other kid treasures in that sweet corner, with enough counter space above it for them to work. It has made helping and being in the kitchen more inviting and enjoyable for them. In other words, I think it has made it feel like home. This was an area the kids were able to look forward to as we were demolishing the only kitchen we knew in the hopes of replacing it with something better and more meaningful.

For me, I didn't come up with something to build into the kitchen and instead decided that what I wanted was my own little drawer with a well-stocked supply of quality, healthy chocolates. So, in our new kitchen, my little piece of heaven is the permission to restock my sweets whenever they run low. The rest of the family knows this is Mama's space. I get to choose when to share, so I don't get surprised by an empty drawer in the midst of a chocolate craving. In fact, I'm going to go get a piece of chocolate right now…

Since we have little ones, we place items at kids' level that they can access themselves. For example, in the kitchen, we have a bottom drawer stocked with kid lunch items: fruit squeezes, bars, cookie bags, chips, pretzels, etc. Then, in a lower part of the freezer, there are sandwiches, or the kids can reach the bread and sandwich fixings. The family room, which we call the fun room, has a play area with a table and bookshelf that are kid-sized.

A space for each person

Choosing Core Styles

A deliberate aspect of a home is picking a style or set of styles you like. Different styles have varying roof lines, architectural elements and floor layouts, so they become relevant during a remodel, not just when we get talking about interior design, decor and furniture.

From Joanna Gaines' book *Homebody*: Six foundational design styles—Farmhouse, Rustic, Modern, Industrial, Traditional, and Boho—offer guideposts for figuring out what makes a space feel like "you." *Farmhouse* charms with nostalgic warmth and welcoming textures; *Rustic* leans into raw, natural materials; *Modern* brings clean lines and simplicity; *Industrial* wears exposed metal, concrete, and practicality with boldness; *Traditional* carries history, craftsmanship, and time-honored elegance; and *Boho* layers stories, color, texture, and eclectic soul. Gaines' best advice? Homes don't have to fit neatly in a box. Mix and match up to 3 core styles to make it your own while still having a space that feels cohesive and makes sense. [2]

In our home, one of the styles we chose is traditional because of the craftsmanship and age of the house. Otherwise, we would be fighting the house all along the way. Dave also likes traditional, and I appreciate the timeless, tried and true side of it. We also both like modern, and a rustic, old-world feel is our 3rd. Sometimes we may come across a piece we really like that pulls boho, and both of us like those industrial coffee shops, but in our own home, we intentionally resist. When we want to sip a cup of joe in a cool modern industrial setting, to a local coffee shop we go. In our own home, we want to feel cozy. By being intentional about the core styles, we keep the home from simply becoming eclectic.

Intentionality Looks Good

We stayed in an Airbnb for a Christian women's business mastermind, and I noticed how homey it felt. Sterling, our hostess, brought in two or three pieces of artwork of faith that were on topic for our meeting, making it personalized and relevant to our event. The home itself was functional, intentional, and beautiful. The owners of the Airbnb had thought through what people would be doing in each space and added the little touches to accommodate. There was a fitted wood piece on the arm of the couch to provide a place to put a drink, a soft ottoman to kick your feet up, and comfy blankets. The colors were cohesive, and the furnishings were comfortable. They had put their love and work into this. It felt so good to be in that space

---

2   Joanna Gaines, *Homebody: A Guide to Creating Spaces You Never Want to Leave* (New York: Harper Collins, 2020).

because someone had taken the time to think through and accommodate our needs, and the personalized touches for our group were created in minutes.

Another example of intentionality hangs in our hallway coat closet. The kitchen counter was a constant struggle to keep clean, so I thought through what tended to end up mindlessly plopped down on the focal point of our kitchen. It was usually mail, Dave's work schedule, kids' spelling words for the week, a magazine, keys, Dave's wallet, and cell phones. So when we redesigned the coat closet, I added a rustic wood shelf with black modern hardware onto the wall. It has key rings on the bottom, a small shelf to hold a wallet and cell phones, and a magazine holder for the paperwork. There is still the daily task of sorting mail and going through the kids' schoolwork, but now, when it's done, those items that are still needed to reference have a place to go that's accessible while being out of the way. Win!

With each room, before mindlessly filling it with couches or furnishings, try to think through what the room offers and how that would best serve you. For example, the family room has a fireplace, south-facing windows, and is open to the dining room and kitchen. This makes for a sunny, cozy space, especially in the cooler and darker winter months. We put the deep, comfortable couches here. One of the thoughtful decisions for this room was regarding a TV. The obvious place was on the mantle above the fireplace, but this would have been the centerpiece of not only the family room but the dining room and kitchen as well. It would have dominated the beautiful stone fireplace and hearth and begged to be on. We didn't want the most-used areas of our home to be TV-centric. However, we do sometimes like to have the news on in the background or a Sunday afternoon football game, and there are special occasions when we'll watch a family show during dinner. What we ended up doing is putting a frame TV that looks like artwork or family pictures when it's off. This way, it doesn't look or feel like a TV unless we are using it as such.

Tip: Spend the money on stuff you use a lot. If you eat together, the dining table is typically used daily, if not multiple times a day. It's okay to make the effort here. Items we touch every day like door knobs are typically not that expensive and get a good bang for buck.

The Value of Spending "Ugly Money" on that Which is Unseen

Some home upgrades don't look pretty but make a huge difference in comfort and peace of mind. For example, we installed a hot water recirculation line because it took a long time to get hot water in our upstairs master bathroom from the water heater in the opposite end of the basement. At first, I hesitated to spend on something unseen, but after we did, it made daily life better and my face cleaner.

While new bathrooms and kitchens look great, don't neglect the systems that keep your home running. Beautiful finishes add charm, but a working water heater adds real warmth to a home.

Our relative Joseph's parents spent thousands of dollars renovating the half bathroom of their home, all while ignoring the water heater that was so old, it barely produced enough heat for 1 person to take a quick shower. Yes we get to enjoy the beauty of those very visible upgrades, but it's also valuable to remember those items that simply make the home work better. Yes a new bathroom is pretty, but will it really bring the peace we long for when we're concerned about the water tank going out and not having the funds left to take care of it if and when that happens? Pretty finishes that you can see add warmth and personality, but a hot water heater adds warmth and peace in an entirely different way.

The associated principle is the value of the unseen. Would you want a beautiful home without running water or without sinks and faucets hooked up to water and drains? Would you want a lovely, meaningful painting without warm water for the shower? Obviously these are extreme examples, but they make a point. It can be hard to spend money on those items for our homes that no one will see, but they can go just as far, and sometimes farther, than beautiful elements.

Technology

While there have been lovely homes for centuries without modern tech, we do have options available to us today that can add safety, convenience, interest and fun to our homes. Here are a few practical ways we've integrated technology to serve us in daily life.

1. **Home Security**—We installed a Vivint security system that lets us automate door locks, receive alerts if doors or the garage are left open, and monitor packages with front porch cameras. Features like 'deter mode' help prevent porch theft. Number lock pads on all entrances allow easy access without keys. You can arm or disarm the system remotely via phone, adding convenience, peace of mind, and occasional opportunities for good pranks. This security system provides an extra feeling of security, especially when I am home alone with the kids.

2. **Smart Lights**—These are relatively inexpensive and can simply be screwed into an existing lamp or fixture, so it's super easy. The Wiz lights, for example, have a Circadian Rhythm setting that I like since the lights will automatically adjust based on the time of day, so you don't get blasted with bright lights right before bed. Right now, since it's early in the morning, I have them in a cozy setting with the brightness turned up enough to work. The kids like the "party lights" that change colors each at different times, and since we installed 6 can smart lights in the living room, they can put out quite an array! There are Christmas settings, Romance lights, Fall, Focus lights, and lots more. They can be set on schedules or on vacation mode to simulate people being home. And they can be controlled with your voice using Amazon Alexa or Google Home.

3. **HVAC** – we have two tablet-style screens instead of a basic thermostat to control the HVAC units in the house. Since the two A/C units are synced, we can control the upstairs and downstairs units from either screen. It has easy modes like summer or spring or away mode. If I want to open the French doors to the backyard on a pretty day, I can easily set a temporary temperature before the units kick on and air conditions the great outdoors from the dining room. It tells me the humidity levels, the temperature outside, and is set to show a picture as the screen saver. As you would expect, this also syncs to an app on the phone where we can control the settings from almost anywhere.

4. **Laundry** – The smart washer/dryer set also syncs to the phone so we can be notified when the laundry is ready. There's an overnight setting that prioritizes energy efficiency over completing the cycle sooner. There are modes called "Fresh Care" on the washer and dryer that gently toss the clothes periodically so that wrinkles don't set if we aren't going to pull out the laundry as soon as the machine finishes. Laundry isn't my favorite, but it is nicer with the extra help from tech.

Appliances: Invest Where it Counts

Some appliances are worth splurging on, and some you can balance with budget-friendly options.

1. **The Steam Oven**—Our steam oven has been a total workhorse. It bakes, roasts, steams, and never dries out food—a great investment for anyone who actually likes eating what they cook.

2. **The PRO48 Fridge**—Then there's the PRO48, our ode to Dave. We didn't buy it to impress anyone; we bought it because we love it. Backlit compartments, massive drawers, a fridge that feels like a Ferrari for the kitchen. Let this serve as a reminder that you get to do it your way.

Do it your way

3. **A Practical Tip**—Designer Joanna Gaines nails it: To elevate the style of a kitchen, invest in a high-end stove, and balance the rest of the appliance suite with more budget-friendly options. This provides function, longevity, and style all in one, without breaking the bank on everything else.

The Pretty Parts that are Seen

There's a balance between fashion and function, and the energy put into thinking through both parts is well spent. For example, we looked at some beautiful faucets for the kitchen that made my heart go pitter patter. One was an antique style that mounted to the wall or the back of the sink if the back was tall enough, with a beautiful decorative hook for the hose to hang on and a romantic metal sprayer. From a fashion standpoint, it was my first choice. So charming.

It did not end up being what we chose for our kitchen. Dave compared it to a 1970s remodeled F-100 pickup (my dream car by the way). He said it's very cool, but do you want it as your daily driver? So what we ended up choosing instead for our main kitchen faucet is a sleek Delta touch faucet with a retractable sprayer and with a small sensor that lights up blue if the water is cool, yellow if it's warm, and red if it's hot. With small kids especially, this makes it easy to teach them to check the temperature first. I'll log away the idea of that sexy decorative faucet for if there's ever somewhere that it won't be used often. The Delta faucets are still nice, pretty, and seamless with the style of our kitchen. You can still 100% make a different choice than we did and choose the gorgeous faucet.

Since our kitchen styles are modern, rustic, and traditional, we went with a modern faucet for the functionality and put in rustic elements up a little higher…

Where we did focus more on fashion is the 2 decorative sconces above the sink – we picked super cute copper light fixtures that draw the eye up and steal the show from the faucets. Ah, a balance of beauty and functionality. This is a great place for "pops of money." Spending a little extra on the higher end light fixtures in a focal area of the kitchen is well worth it. We also put in a beautiful, decorative wooden ledge on either side of the sink. This gives us less storage cabinets, but it also opens up the kitchen and is simply gorgeous.

Another place where we put in time and money for something pretty is the cabinets on each side of the stove. We chose custom water glass cabinet doors with leaded accents on the top and bottom. We also lit these cabinets and put in glass shelving. Again, it's a focal point in the kitchen where we gave up a little functionality, and it has been well worth it.

Beautiful pillars of light

God at the Center

The rest of the story about these beautiful rain glass cabinets is the spiritual significance they hold. How do we put God at the center of our home? Pray about it and ask Him! At one point in the middle of the remodel, I was questioning several elements of our kitchen. I prayed about it and then felt there was one element still left to change that He would guide us on. I felt like we had considered each member of the family, creating a special place for each person to love, but had not yet included Him. I felt like this last missing piece (that was also causing me to miss my "peace") would be something that made me think of God and reminded me to glorify Him in this space when I saw it. It would be easy to ignore or push through this feeling instead of honoring it, but fortunately I let myself both rest in it and wrestle with it. Then about a week later, an image came to me of the 2 glass cabinets lit up like 2 pillars of light. I saw glass in front of it that looked like water, reminding us that He is the living water, as well as being a reminder of baptism, the water through which we are purified.

We found a rain glass, and our designer sketched a little leaded design on the top and bottom that subtly looks like a sideways cross. We use it as the nightlight in the kitchen, lighting up the darkness when nothing else is on, and shining His light upon us. Now I feel this calm that it is complete. They say the kitchen is the heartbeat of the home, and now He has given us a way to bring His light, His living water into the center because we were seeking Him. He says, "seek and You shall find," and He means what He says. We can take Him at His word.

Why do we need to put God at the center of our home and lives? We are reminded in the Psalms that, "Unless the Lord builds the house, They labor in vain who build it; Unless the Lord guards the city, The watchman keeps awake in vain." My grandfather used to say, "Work like everything depends on you. Pray like everything depends on God." While I don't think he was the one who wrote that phrase, that was how I learned of it. Again in His word, we are reminded that, "We can make our plans, but the LORD determines our steps." When a remodel isn't going quite how we thought, that is such a powerful reminder to surrender it to Him, to accept that maybe this is the perfect path even if it wasn't exactly as we planned it, and to have peace.

Fashion and Function

The backsplash in the kitchen is the same beautiful, smooth, modern quartz we have on the countertops. This checks the function and fashion boxes since we find it quite pretty while still being easy to clean, especially by the stove where it gets splashed with grease and can simply be wiped down. There isn't always a tradeoff.

Having beautiful places to rest my eyes in our own home truly makes a difference. Often these are finishing design touches like furniture and decor, which we'll discuss more in the design simplified chapter. There are also abundant opportunities to build these into our homes as we remodel or build.

Rest Your Eyes

Bits of Joy, even in the Middle of a Remodel

For me, what I didn't want was for our kids (or us for that matter) to remember this remodel season of life as a time when we were stressed out and no fun to be around. I wanted them to remember it as an adventure and something special. From that mindset came the solution that accomplished that goal.

Find a way to make the Journey an adventure – does that mean camping out in the house? Do we move out to a spot with something special like a swimming pool? We came up with a combination that fit our circumstances:

First, for the month of August, we moved into an apartment with a fantastic swimming pool and hot tub. We went swimming 5-6 days a week. The kids had a ball, and it sure helped to lighten the mood for Dave and I, too. Then in the month of September, since the pool would be closing, we moved in with some friends who had a full apartment in their basement. The kids got to have lots of playdates, and the moms got special visits that just wouldn't have happened otherwise. That came with its own challenges of having a shared space, but those challenges I think were invisible to the kids, and it came with unique benefits too. When I told the kids we were moving back home in two weeks, Cole said "Aw, I want to stay with our friends! We get to have play dates every day." Mission accomplished.

Essentials Over Upgrades

One huge aha moment for me was realizing the difference between necessities and upgrades. Basics and finishing touches come first—safety fixes, repairs, and anything that makes your home feel *done*. Once those are in place, you can rest in the peace of a finished home.

Upgrades? Those are optional, endless, and fun—but not required. We treat them like dessert: a laundry room redo for us goes into the "when we're bored and there's lots of money in the bank" category.

Before we figured this out, we sometimes splurged on upgrades only to realize parts of the house still felt unfinished. Mentally, we'd act like every little item had to be done now, when in reality it was just another optional upgrade. The key: finish the essentials first, then enjoy upgrades on your own timeline.

Key Takeaways

- Plan Resources: Budget your home renovation to include all the expenses, like holding costs or paying rent if you move out for a period of time, and include a healthy buffer.

- Focus on Flow and Function: Pay attention to practical aspects like walkway widths, appliance placement (microwave height, refrigerator clearance), and kitchen layout (triangle). These impact daily living and long-term satisfaction.

- Measure and Visualize Before Making Changes: Accurately measure furniture and fixtures to ensure they fit the space, and consider taping off areas to visualize the layout. This helps avoid costly mistakes and ensures proper scale.

- Balance Aesthetics with Practical Upgrades: While pretty finishes are important, don't neglect "unseen" improvements like HVAC systems or hot water recirculation, which enhance comfort and daily living.

- Consider Future Needs and Personalization: Think about how your needs will change in the coming years and ensure renovations can adapt. Personalize spaces to reflect individual interests, making it truly everyone's home.

- Prioritize Essentials Over Optional Upgrades: Complete necessary repairs and finishing touches before getting caught up in "extras." This creates a sense of completion and peace in your home.

Chapter 8

Design Simplified

Design isn't just about ticking off furniture items and interior decor. It's about creating spaces that you feel good in and that support your lifestyle and the things you love to do. In this chapter, first we'll talk about a completely different way of looking at design, and that's through the lens of joy!

We'll also cover lots of design tips and strategies. Design "rules" are not here to limit us, they're here as a guide because they are what tends to look appropriate and cohesive, which calms the nervous system and brings peace. They can be very empowering, because they give us the tools to problem solve why a space might not be working or might be clashing with itself. Then we can resolve those discrepancies and enjoy the beauty that comes with it.

Designing for Joy

Ingrid Fetell Lee designs for joy. A concept I learned from her is to look at a room and ask "What do I want to happen in this space?" She said we tend to look at a living room, for example, and think of a checklist of furnishings that "belong" in a living room: couch, coffee table, lamp, etc. She suggested that instead we ask "How do I create a space where the things I want to have happen actually happen?"

The Fun Room: Where the Foundational Elements and Beauty Meet

There was this big coffee table in our living room. We used to move it every now and then to get space to do other things like reclining the sofa, dancing or playing with toys. Ironically, we never used to drink coffee on it. When we eventually removed it, our living room magically transformed into a 'fun room' where the kids dance and play freely. This taught me to design spaces for real-life use, not just tradition.

Exercise

If it feels far off still, take a moment to imagine and hope.

Pick a space in your home that you want to make memories in:

____

What kind of moments do you want to create in that space? Feel free to dream, play, imagine, and even be a little silly here. You can always throttle it back later. ____

____

____

____

What changes to the space or what furniture would help create those moments? Is there anything to remove? What about to add? _______________

____

____

Our home is a canvas for joy. That takes some of the pressure off making the home perfect. An example Ingrid Fetell Lee gave is Dr. Becky, a designer and author who doesn't like her floors, but they're great for racing cars, so she tapes them up to make roads and great memories with her toddler. That brings joy! Here, she has made a little trade off, giving a little on the "beauty" side in exchange for the functional element of floors that make good racetracks and the foundational element of loving, serving and enjoying her boys. What a joyful choice!

She suggests viewing your home as a collection of meaningful moments. Instead of a checklist of furniture to buy, instead look at the moments we create and want to create. Think of the memories we share and will share here. Doesn't that feel good? For me, it takes some pressure off having to buy certain stuff that everyone else thinks I need and gives me permission to make it our own.[3]

Maya Angelou said, "I've learned that people will forget what you said, people will forget what you did, but people will never forget how you made them feel." I think the same concept can be applied to our homes. People will forget what the artwork on the walls looks like, people will forget if the toys were out of place, but people will remember how the home made them feel. For example, does it feel welcoming and happy, or are we concerned with making everything just right the whole time? Personally, I still drift back into old habits once in a while, but when I think about it and am intentional, I can choose to let go of perfection so that my family, our guests, and I can have an outstanding time.

Order is also grounding, but we can think of that with joy too. For example, we put 3 bins with pops of color in a row with all the toys in them. The toys are still accessible. It's not a tug of war between kids and parents where we

---

3   "Embracing Joy in Motherhood: Lessons Learned for Mother's Day," last modified May 2023, accessed on December 21, 2024, https://jyo.world/awareness/embracing-joy-in-motherhood-lessons-learned-for-mothers-day/

hide all the kids' stuff. Everyone should have ownership of the home like they really live there. There are ways to find a balance so it feels like a home everyone lives in.

It used to feel like I would lose and the kids would win every time I would choose a kid item for a space instead of a pretty item for me. Not anymore. I love these kids and enjoy them. Some of our best memories are when I've finally gotten myself to get out of my own world and enter theirs. Now seeing the items that bring them joy mixed in makes this our Murphy home. I've also learned to get pretty kids items that I like looking at, so everyone wins.

Kids and Adults Win

As seasons of life change, whatever that looks like for each of us, our home will adapt with us. I already know the small bookshelf of toys that's just the right size for toddlers will one day have run its course for us, and it will make way for the next exciting piece. Just like the people living in it, our home grows and changes. But as long as the love and the welcome is here, as long as we like how it looks and feels, it will serve us in every season.

Tip: Ask yourself, "What memories do I want to make in this room?" Then make the choices about what to do with the space, as well as what to put in it and what to take out, based on that decision. For example, it's easy to put a couch, coffee table, and TV in a living room. That creates a space where the primary activities are watching TV and sipping drinks. That might be what you want, to cuddle up on the couch and kick back for the evening. If you would rather have more memories of dancing in the living room, playing on the floor, and cozying up with a blanket by the fireplace, consider either removing the TV or making it more subtle (like a frame TV that displays artwork, putting it in a less central spot, or covering it with barn doors for example). You may also want to leave out the coffee table and just use end tables to make space on the floor.

The Value of Beauty

Beauty has innate value. I'm a practical girl and used to undervalue beauty. Yet look how beautiful God made his creation for us to enjoy. Women are uniquely made to reflect the beauty of God, first in ourselves by reflecting that feminine, beautiful side of our creator, and then by the ways beyond ourselves that we bring beauty into the world. Our home is a central place where we bring that beauty, our own little place in the world that we get to create to reflect who we are and the innate beauty in ourselves. Men are drawn to that beauty and also enjoy it. Creating order is also appealing, although we may not call it beautiful, but it is aesthetically pleasing.

Beauty can also be personal. When I first considered switching from simple modern black lights to the chandeliers I kept craving, it felt vulnerable because it's what I truly like. The modern lights are safe. Everyone likes those, and if they don't, I can hide behind the fact that they're simply modern and trending. But the chandeliers were a bold statement of me, Maya Murphy, and the beauty I actually like. They simght not be everyone's style. At the same time that it felt vulnerable, it also felt authentic, and that made it worth it. It's funny to think that it takes courage to choose beauty that is truly us.

It doesn't escape me that the day we thought of removing the coffee table, the day our living room became the fun room, was the day our designer Megan came through. She added three substantial mirrors on the wall and a spacious, comfortable rug on the ground. With those new beautiful additions, I could envision the space being used to dance instead of to sit and watch TV or drink coffee. Improving the design led to re-envisioning what the room could be. After she left, I remember us sitting down in our home and just soaking in how much better it felt.

An easy change that packs a big punch is new couch pillows. My cousin Nori had been considering replacing hers to refresh the room, and her husband didn't understand why. Then, when she swapped them out, he came to believe. Even the skeptical husband couldn't deny the difference. It renewed the room and made it enjoyable to be in again. It was a simple design change, but it was powerful.

Simple renewal

For me, designing wasn't something that came naturally at first, but I have come to realize and appreciate just how impactful it can be when the colors and styles make sense together. I have seen it be that difference between a room that just feels good and one that, for some reason, doesn't quite work with itself. I have also learned how to design a beautiful room I love. If I can learn it, anyone can! Adding in those personal touches, not just in style but in choices and items that tell our story and have meaning to us, brings it all together to feel homey.

Twenty Design Golden Nuggets

1. **Metals** – Be consistent, or if you choose a couple metals for a space, make sure you like how they match together. For example, oil-rubbed bronze and copper go well together. Before we learned this, our bedroom just didn't feel right because there were clashing metals. Once we became aware of it and changed to consistent metals, the whole room felt more peaceful and beautiful.

Metals and Bold Colors

2.   **Bold Colors** – Bold colors can make a room feel moody and sophisticated. If you have a color you love and gravitate towards, you can make that the accent color for the room or even a pop color throughout the home. Then use more neutrals around it. The bold colors will be more stimulating and exciting, so consider more of this in rooms that you want to be invigorating or that you won't be in for long periods of time such as a workout space or bathroom. With trends moving this direction right now, this is a fun way to change the feel of a space. Designer Joanna Gaines has said many times she would wonder if she went too dark only to find that once the paint dries, not once has it seemed too dark after all.

3.   **Neutral Colors** – Bright, lighter colors make a room feel open and airy. They are also less stimulating, so it's more relaxing. To keep them from being boring or feeling like a hospital, avoid a stark white and instead choose a white more like shiplap. White is the trickiest color, so pay attention to undertones that pull warm, grey, yellow, etc. Hold the whites your considered against a true white to be able to see the nuance of it, or go with a white that's tried and true, like a bestseller or one that a designer you love uses. Feel free to take your time and see it in different lighting. Since neutral and lighter colors are less stimulating, this may be preferred in bedrooms and more restful spaces. Remember, you get to choose how you feel in your home, so you can go with bolder or more neutral elements.

Neutral Colors

4. **Textures** – This is a fun way to bring contrast and interest without making it overstimulating. Designers are so good at this! You can have several throw pillows on a couch that are similar colors, for example, but if the textures have stark contrast, it will still be interesting.

Textures create interest

5. **Odd Numbers** – Generally, having one large piece of decor, 3, 5, or 7 pieces works better than even numbers. For example, on the mantle above the fireplace, you may have 3 pieces on 1 side and 2 pieces on the other.

Odd Numbers

6. **Stand Back and Look** – We can use these as a rule of thumb. Then just stand back and look at it. If it doesn't look right, try something else. This is fun because it brings in the sizes, shapes, and nuances of each piece without having to understand it all and just knowing when it looks good together.

Stand Back and Look

7. **Spacing and Angles** – Don't squish the décor together. My husband will take the pieces on the dining table — salt and pepper shakers, a vase, a napkin holder — and push them all into one tight cluster. Let pieces breathe. Giving items space between them instantly makes a surface feel calmer and more intentional.

    But spacing isn't the only detail that matters. Pay attention to angles. If a chair is placed against a wall or bay window, notice whether the back of the chair lines up with the angle behind it. When the lines compete — even slightly — the whole room can feel subtly "off." Simply adjusting a piece so it aligns with the architecture can solve the problem in seconds. Sometimes a space doesn't need new furniture — it just needs a small turn.

Space between decor

8. **Art Height** – When hanging pictures or art on the walls, Tidbitsandtwine.com describes a good rule of thumb of putting the center of the art at eye level (57-60" from the ground) with standard 8 foot ceilings. Try adjusting to 60" with 9 foot ceilings and 62" for 10 foot ceilings, even up to 63" if ceilings are taller than 10 feet. Use tip six here: remember to stand back and look. If

hanging a few pieces of varying sizes, make sure the center of each is at eye level (avoid aligning frames so the tops or bottoms are all at the same height if they are different sizes). When hanging a group of art where each is the same size, think of them as 1 single piece and space them evenly throughout, with the middle hung at eye level. When hanging artwork over a couch or console table, generally space it 8" above the top of the furniture so the pieces feel connected, although anywhere between 6-10" may work depending on the height of the furniture.[4]

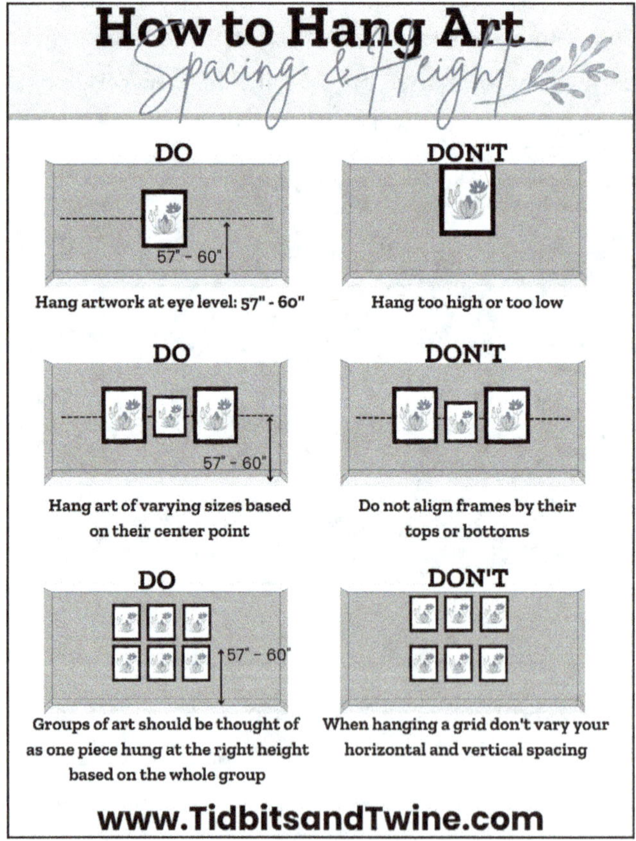

4   "How High to Hang Pictures: Everything You Need to Know," last modified October 15, 2023, accessed November 7, 2024, https://www.tidbitsandtwine.com/how-high-to-hang-pictures/.

9. **Making a Room Feel Taller** – There are a few visual effects that can help create the illusion of height in a room with standard or low ceilings. One idea we incorporated in the living room is painting the trim the same color as the walls. By not having several inches of white at the bottom of the wall, it makes the walls feel taller. Another tip is bringing curtains almost all the way up to the ceiling. The extra length of the curtains again extends the perceived height of the ceilings. A third trick that blew me away with how much it did is adding a low profile trim to the ceiling. Wow, we did this when we remodeled the basement guest bathroom, and it went from feeling like a low, cramped room to feeling tall and open. Vertical lines can also increase the perceived height.

Create Height

10. **Hanging Curtains** – Curtains are typically hung above the trim around the window by three to six inches, and the curtain rod

usually extends six inches past the window trim on each side. Since there are usually 2 curtain panels, each one is half the rod length. For the length of the curtains, the most common design is to have the curtains "kiss" the floor. This is accomplished by measuring from the top of the rod down to the floor, with minor adjustments to account for the hanging method. It's not overkill to measure a couple times. This is just a rule of thumb and gives you a guide that will look appropriate. Remember though, this is your home, and there are no design police. The previous tip suggested hanging curtains higher for a different effect, so even here you get to choose what you like.[5]

Curtains often kiss the floor

11. **Pops of Color** – Several versions of this principle exist from different top designers. One is the pops of red theory, that you can add a little spark of red in the form of a pillow, lamp or other small item, into a space to create interest and make a statement. If you lean more neutral with the overall design of a room, this is an easy and powerful way to create interest. This can also be used to

---

5   Mari Herrema, "How to choose and hang curtains, according to an interior design expert," November 17, 2021, accessed November 7, 2024,

decorate for the holidays, swapping out couch pillows and the like for colorful seasonal options. Since the pops are bolder elements, if you get tired of them, no problem! It's easy to change.[6] You don't have to design this way, but it is an option.

Pops of Color

12. **Bringing the Outdoors In** - One of the highlights in our guest bathroom has turned out to be the river rock floors. They are so fun! This small basement bathroom with no windows feels like a walk outside or like walking into a spa. It's amazing how those sliced river rocks and the rain style showerhead bring the outdoors in. They're

---

6   Emily Kammerlohr, "12 Color Rules Joanna Gaines Swears By," June 17, 2023, accessed July 13, 2024, https://www.housedigest.com/1315297/paint-color-rules-hgtv-joanna-gaines-swears-by/. https://www.businessinsider.com/guides/home/how-to-hang-curtains#:~:text=How%20to%20choose%20and%20hang%20curtains%2C%20according%20to,the%20rod%20with%20the%20curtains%20already%20on%20it.

also timeless elements, since nature isn't a trend. Light and bright colors, coupled with plants, also help bring the outdoors in a way that feels light and airy.

13. **The Power of Plants** – The science is mounting about the benefits of having plants in our homes. Studies have found that live indoor plants reduce stress, sharpen attention, offer therapeutic benefits, speed up recovery from illness, boost productivity, improve job satisfaction, and increase air quality.[7] They're also simply beautiful and make a room come alive. Some varieties are incredibly easy to care for: I had an aloe vera live a year without even dirt or water, and a pothos plant can simply be placed in water. A part of your pothos plant can also be snipped off and will regrow roots into a whole new plant.

Pothos plant

---

7 Rebeccah Joy Stanborough, "A Hobby for All Seasons: 7 Science-Backed Benefits of Indoor Plants" September 18, 2020, accessed November 7, 2024, https://www.healthline.com/health/healthy-home-guide/benefits-of-indoor-plants.

14. **Fabric Placement** - I like to generally put fabrics that stain easily in places that don't get dirty as fast. For example, white curtains are easier to keep clean than a white couch. I've seen a gorgeous new white couch already looked a little dingy simply because blue jeans can transfer color onto the fabric. None of this means you *can't* choose white or light fabrics in high wear places. You absolutely can! Just decide if the extra cleaning and wear is worth it to you. For the white plush bathmats I really wanted, I decided the extra washing was ok with me.

15. **Swap the Elements** - If you see a room you love, don't feel pressure to recreate it exactly. Designers rarely copy a space piece-for-piece. Instead, they identify the key elements — texture, contrast, color, shape — and then move those elements around in a new way. Maybe the inspiration room has leather pillows and white curtains; you might use a leather chair and white art instead. By swapping elements rather than duplicating them, you capture the same feeling without chasing the exact items.

16. **Furniture for Real Life** - Choose materials that match how your family actually lives. We picked cloth chairs and a wooden bench for our dining table because we enjoy sipping coffee together at the table and lingering in conversation with guests after a meal. These days, many fabrics are made to resist stains and wipe clean with just a damp cloth. Other times, darker tones or patterned fabrics that hide spills and dirt simply bring more peace to your daily life. There's no "right" choice—you get to decide what supports the way you live and the home you want to create.

White Desk and Leather Chair

17. **Warm/Cool Undertones** - Colors almost always have an undertone, meaning they lean either **warm (cream/yellow)** or **cool (grey/blue)**. When the main elements in a space share the same undertone, the room feels naturally cohesive and calm. On the other hand, when undertones fight each other - like a cool grey tile next to a warm creamy paint - the room can feel "off," even if every piece is beautiful on its own. Some finishes are chameleons and can go either way. For example, wood floors that include both warm brown tones and hints of black or grey can bridge the gap between warm and cool. Once your eye is trained to notice undertones, you'll start to see why certain spaces feel effortless and pulled together and why others never quite feel right, no matter how much you decorate. Quick trick: Compare the color next to bright white like a piece of printer paper. If it suddenly looks creamy, it's warm. If it looks bluish or dull, it's cool.

Warm Undertones

18. **Three Matching Elements** - One of the easiest ways to make a room feel cohesive is to repeat the same finish, material, or color in at least three places. When a detail shows up only once, it can feel random or like it doesn't belong. When it shows up twice, it starts to feel intentional. But when it shows up three times, the room suddenly feels "pulled together," even if everything else is simple. It can be something small, like black accents, warm wood tones, brass hardware, woven textures, or a certain shade of blue. It's a subtle design trick, but it creates a sense of harmony that your eyes can feel, even if you can't explain why.

Repeat matching elements

19. **Take Your Time** – Good design rarely happens in a rush. In the beginning, if I didn't find the right piece within a few minutes, I assumed I just wasn't good at it. But I noticed that talented designers often spend hours thinking through a room before making decisions. When I released the pressure to finish quickly, the process became creative and even enjoyable. I began thinking about the room as a whole instead of one piece at a time — and I realized I actually could design.

20. **Budgeting Design Overall** - Try to look at your budget as a whole instead of the cost of each item individually. Sometimes it takes spending way too much on one item because that piece is what rounds out the room. Maybe in one case, the pillows on the couch end up being very inexpensive, but in another situation, the pillows end up being costly because it's the perfect size, fabric, and shape to pull the space together. Either way is just fine as long as you set a budget and work toward that number overall. In our entryway, the perfect rustic bench was a pricey vintage piece, but the other elements were economical enough to make up for it and keep us on budget.

Entryway with Rustic Bench

The Home Keys

1. Personal – a reflection of the people living in it. What they like and value, where they've been and where they're going, their roots.

2. Functional – it works. The layout, a place to put your drink and phone, comfortable without the sun glaring in your eyes, etc.

3. Beautiful – cohesive and appealing to the eye. In harmony with itself.

Is a Rug Worth it?

For at least a couple decades of my life, I would have said no. I would have seen no functional value and underestimated the value the beauty would bring. But now I see it differently, and let me tell you why.

As I looked around, I began to think maybe there was a reason so many people put rugs in their homes. There's a reason stores have a rug with each living room display. Open to the idea of getting one, we found a beautiful, Turkish-style, faded blue rug at a big sale. Every time I look at it, the design draws me in, which helps make our space more personal. It takes an otherwise loud, echoey room and helps mute it to a more pleasant volume, increasing the functionality. It defines the space in an otherwise simple, long rectangular room, making the whole area more beautiful. The threads sit low enough that the vacuum goes over it without getting stuck on the edges. And since it's good quality, it would last and be easy to clean.

Inviting Rug

When we laid the rug in the center of the living room, something happened that exceeded my expectations. The kids suddenly flocked to the room. Cole lay on the floor on the cozy rug, and Amora started twirling and dancing on it. This soft, inviting surface gave them a safe space to play in a room that had long been ignored. The rug made this space feel like home. Since then, this rug has been the backdrop for many wrestling matches, spinning contests, picnics, and sitting in front of the fireplace. The baby has lain on the rug surrounded by adoring older siblings and friends.

So it turns out I was wrong for a long time. It turns out a soft rug packs a big punch in turning a house into a home. It also makes a statement decoratively since it covers a large area. It grounds the space and brings the room together. There's an element of completeness with an area rug in the room. If you, like I did, have not seen the value of a rug until now, go ahead and find one that's soft enough to lie on and low enough to the ground so no one trips on the edge.

A Harmony of Items

I finally did it. After a few months of stalling out, making excuses about each potential decorative purchase Nori showed me, in a moment of clarity, I said yes to ordering a few items for the family room. We ordered wallpaper, a wooden tray, and two poufs. When the wooden tray with the faux leather handles arrived, it was love at first sight. The grainy dark wood is beautiful, the curves in the round tray are warm, and the leather handles give it a clean rustic touch.

That was an easy decision. A few days later, two large boxes arrived on the front porch with the poufs. The kids excitedly helped me take them out, and with the two-foot by two-foot poufs still wrapped in plastic, they quickly found ways to play with them. My first impression of the poufs however was that I didn't like them. In fact, I think I even said it out loud. But something I've noticed is that when I look at a space that's well put together, it's often not the individual pieces that draw me to it. It's the collaboration, the harmony of the elements together that create a certain feel. So it seems to be with these poufs and the beauty they bring in by tying the room together.

After getting the kids to bed that evening, I came downstairs to have a little time in the family room. The boxes and plastic-wrapped poufs were still out in the middle of the Living Room, partially by design so I could keep glancing over and getting a feel for what I think of them. Out of a desire for functionality, I unwrapped the plastic. I wanted to be able to prop my feet up on one of them while sitting on the couch and also wanted to be able to put a cup of tea on that beautiful wood tray on the other. Once they were unwrapped, the blue braided burlap stitched in and out of the edges popped, and how well it matched the couches and rug stood out. Hmm, I like these more. The idea in my mind is that the material would be too rough, but as I sit here with bare feet propped up on the pouf, it's quite comfortable. Because of the rustic burlap style intertwined with an earthy blue, these will handle wear and tear well (good news in a home with kids). So the functionality of them keeping up with the kiddos is also appealing.

So poufs, I take back all those bad things I said about you. Not every item has to make our hearts go pitter patter. Like the harmony of a band, each piece does its part to add to the whole (that's why we don't often hear tuba solos, but that deep tone adds an important element).

A Harmony of Items

Decorating for Holidays

If you knew how little I did, you'd probably laugh at the fact that this is even a section in this book. It's here for a reason though, because even when the changes are small and simple, when they're in central locations like on the mantle, dining table, or kitchen island, they pack a big punch. They give our home a rhythm, and it is fun.

For fall, maybe I get a small bag with half a dozen little pumpkins and put them in a bowl in the center of the dining table. I had a pumpkin spice candle that lasted 2 or 3 years, but it marked the scent of the season. As Halloween was approaching, the paper Jack-o-lanterns Cole made would get taped up on the bay doors in the dining room. Our first little Christmas tree stood at an impressive 3 feet tall. These little decorations and smells connected us to the changes happening in the world and the rhythm of life. They brought in the joy of watching the passing time, helping us soak up what each season has to offer.

It's simpler than we sometimes make it, and it's worth it. We can make this fun and go all out, and that's magical too. But we don't even have to do much to capture the essence. It can be a pine candle and an Elf on the Shelf, or a couple seasonal pillows and a simple centerpiece.

Simple Holiday Decor

Tip: When you get Holiday decorations out, box up the normal decorations into the Holiday boxes so your space doesn't feel cluttered. It can be hard to function in a space that is too full, and this balances the items all year round. Perhaps you already do this, but if not, this can be a game changer.

Counsel

If design isn't your thing, there is power in having someone on your team whose thing it is. Proverbs 15:22 says, "Plans fail for lack of counsel, but with many advisers they succeed." That adviser could be a high-end designer, but it doesn't have to be. It could be a friend or family member who loves this stuff and will let you bounce ideas back and forth or help pick out items and organize them beautifully. This is especially nice if the person knows you and has a feel for what you like. It could be a free designer who works for a store where you're purchasing some items for your home, such as cabinets or furnishings.

You don't have to do it all by yourself. The help I've gotten from design-minded people has led to beauty I would not have known how to create on my own. It's still your home. It's still a reflection of you. Be courageous about what you like. That's how you balance it and make sure that it becomes your own instead of just a house where a designer "followed all the rules." Just because they're the expert doesn't mean that they like what you like or know what your gut is telling you. Stand up for what you like and have the courage to be wonderfully you.

Discard the parts that don't fit for you and incorporate the truths that do. Make sure to work with someone who listens and takes the time to understand you. Your home will thank you for it! Remember, you're creating this home to have a safe haven, to have a place of rest, reprieve, and recharge.

The elements of our guest basement bathroom were a culmination of desires and ideas from me, Dave, and our designer, Nori. We each honored what we wanted and knew would work here. Dave wanted black hardware, which contrasts with the cream river rock on the floor. Nori, with her eye for design, knew that putting low-profile but wide crown molding on the ceiling instead of on the top of the wall would make the room look taller. We honored each other while staying true to ourselves. By the time it all came together, it was more beautiful than any of us would have created on our own, because we each had something to add.

Honoring Each Voice

Here for you as some additional guidance is a list of tips for working with a designer. Feel free to use whichever of these tips resonate with you. Remember, at the end of the day, there is no design police!

The Do's and Don'ts of Working with a Designer.

1. Do find a designer that will take the time to learn your style. Our designer Megan Vucich really took the time up front to get a feel for Dave's style and mine. Then by the time she started picking pieces, she had pretty good confidence it would be what we like.

2. Don't settle if what the designer creates doesn't feel like what you envisioned or doesn't feel quite like your style. Even with the time Megan took to understand our style and interests, we still had some back and forth once she sent us renderings. For example, the

rendering she sent for our front living room was very mid-century Modern with heavy pieces of wood furniture. My vision for that room was that it would be light and airy with an open, almost front porch feel. We did go with some of the pieces she chose, but we entirely left out some of the other furnishings. I'm so glad we did!

3. Do trust your gut. You know what you like, and you have intuition.

4. Do ask yourself "what do I want?" You'll see this throughout this book because it bears repeating.

5. Do enjoy the process. Home isn't just a destination, it's a journey too. This is fun stuff.

6. Do take a few short minutes to think about what memories you want to make in a space. Remember your home isn't just a checklist of furnishings, it's a launching pad for amazing memories and a space that serves you in creating the life you want, the life you were built for. Saint Irenaeus said, "the glory of God is man fully alive." You, what you like to do, what you're drawn to, is all a gift to the world. One of the most loving choices you can make for yourself and everyone else is to be true to it.

7. Don't be afraid to make a mistake. There isn't going to be a test, and you can make changes.

8. Do give yourself grace. Before we finished the kitchen remodel, I forgave myself in advance for the things I would learn after a year in the new kitchen that might have led to slightly different choices. And I'm sticking to it. This is for you.

9. Do go for it! There are places in our home where we went for it, where we played all out, like the vision I came up with for our half bath while drinking just a little too much caffeine, and they are some of my favorites!

10. Do give yourself permission to take time and let it simmer. Sometimes when we sleep on it or wait until something feels right, we find the answers that wouldn't have come if we had rushed it.

You can feel it in your body when it's time to go for it, or when something is gently holding you back. Trust it.

Remember that the design "rules" are here to serve and guide. They're a tool available for you, just like having someone on your team who loves design can be such a blessing if that's helpful to you. At the end of the day, just like how we feel different looking at a landscape than the side of a building, bringing beauty into our homes breathes life into our walls.

Key Takeaways

- Prioritize creating spaces that bring joy and facilitate the activities and memories you want to have in your home, rather than just filling rooms with expected furniture or decor. Ask yourself "What do I want to happen in this space?"

- Appreciate that beauty is personal and meaningful. Choose items and designs that resonate with you, whether they are or aren't universally trendy. Authentic beauty, especially through meaningful pieces, contributes to the feeling of home.

- Colors, textures, and layout affect the mood and atmosphere of a room. Use design intentionally to create the feelings you want in your home.

- Embrace Experimentation and Learning. Approach design as a process of discovery. Don't be afraid to make choices and adjustments.

- Working with someone who has a knack for design can help in creating a beautiful space you love, as long as it's balanced with being assertive and staying true to what you like.

Chapter 9

Bringing it All Together

Our homes get to be the place where we recharge, kick our feet up and forget our worries. It's where we can truly be ourselves, even when it's messy, so that it fills us up with joy and prepares us to go out into the world and do the work that God has created us to do. By creating that environment, ""You will go out in joy and be led forth in peace." ~ Isaiah 55:12

We've walked through the excitement of renovations, the establishment of routines, and the discovery of how design impacts our lives. Now, we arrive at a point of integration, where all these threads weave together to form the tapestry of our daily experience.

This chapter is about sustaining the positive changes we've made, finding joy in the present, and navigating the inevitable ebbs and flows of homemaking without losing steam. Let's embark on this last part of our journey, where we learn to appreciate the home we have today and gracefully shape the home we will have tomorrow.

Settle In and Relax

We felt settled into our airBnB the first night we were there. Even our 7 year old commented that it felt like home and that she could tell it was because of me, the work I had done, and what I had learned. Let that serve as evidence that these skills can be learned. You don't have to be born knowing how to create a home; you can practice it.

Step 1: Put things away. A friend of mine would unpack her suitcase in hotel rooms as long as she was staying at least a couple nights, and it's a 10-minute habit I picked up from her. It's incredible how much more rooted and settled it feels to be out of a suitcase. At home, moving out of boxes and finding a permanent place for your things works the same way.

Step 2: Know where things belong. In a vacation rental, this is easy because you only brought the essentials. In your own home, decluttering and assigning systems for your essentials brings clarity and calm.

Step 3: Relax. This was the secret ingredient that made the airBnB feel homey. We didn't think about upgrades or perfection; we just enjoyed the moment. At home, you can do the same. One way to switch into that mindset is to think about what you're experiencing with each of your five senses. Another simple yet powerful technique is to take a slow, deep breath. Allow yourself to appreciate your space as it is.

Exercise

1. Take 3 long, deep breaths. Aah.
2. Notice 4 things you see, 3 things you hear, 2 things you feel, 1 thing you smell. (This brings us back into the present moment).
3. Think of at least 3 aspects of your home you appreciate, whether that's items in it or part of the home itself.

Don't fall into the trap of treating your home as a test you must ace. One friend recently commented that her previous home was "just practice," and the new one had to be done "right." But life happens everywhere: kids grow, friends visit, parties happen, couches get messy. Our homes aren't right or wrong—they're for living.

Tip: Pay attention to how you settle in on vacation, or in any temporary space. What makes you relax? What habits or arrangements make life feel easy? Bring those lessons home like a souvenir—they are guide to creating a space that feels like home, not a project.

When we care for our home, when we take the time to think about our home and how it can be functional to serve us in our day to day lives, how can it be beautiful and pleasing to the eye, and how it can be a reflection of where we've been, what we value, and where we're going in life, then our home "loves" us back. Our home serves those of us living in it and becomes our safe place, a place of rest and recovery, a recharge zone, and a pleasure to be in. We pour in, and then we get filled back up in return.

What If It's Hard?

When we were far enough into the renovation for there to be no turning back, but still far enough away from the finish line to be able to see it starting to come together, I panicked. The question on my mind was, "should it be this hard or am I doing it wrong?"

After talking and praying with my friend Lilly, yes at this point when we're at mile 25 of the marathon and don't know it because the finish line is around the corner and out of sight, yes it can be this hard. It feels so far away still because we can't see it, yet most of the work has been done and so we may be tired. And this is the devil's last chance to try to distract us or keep us from going across the finish, because he knows that as soon as we turn that corner and see the finish line, our energy will be renewed and there will be no coming back. So, the pain is the greatest right now, the questioning is the strongest, and we have the most invested without seeing the payoff yet.

Like labor pains, the closer it gets to victory and completion, the more intense it becomes. This means that soon the hard part will be behind us, and we will have the fruits of our labor. Does having a newborn at home come with challenges and work? Of course, like maintenance on a home, there is continued care, but that care is beautiful and precious, challenging and rewarding. Before becoming a mom, I remember sitting on an airplane next to a dad who was complaining about his children. Not having any of my own and listening to one complaint after another, I finally asked him, "Sooo, if you had it to do over you just would have not had kids then?" His immediate response was, "Are you kidding me?! They're the best thing in the world!"

And so it is that so often in life, the greatest parts require the most effort. The fruits that are hard to reach near the top of the tree are the sweetest, soaked by the sun and untouched.

My friend Lindsey once told me that when we're in the middle of hardship, it can be hard to see if we're handling it well. It doesn't feel like 'success.' But if we do handle it well, one day we look back, and in hindsight, we're able to see just how well we did.

It reminds me of a story I heard an astronaut share. The space shuttle had caught fire, the fire was between him and the extinguisher, and in that moment, he was terrified. But even though the feeling of fear didn't leave him, he continued with what needed to be done, he waded through the flames that were floating through the air in zero gravity, he got the extinguisher, put out the fire, and saved more than just his own life. After it was over, he got a pencil and paper and wrote a note to his young son. It read "Dear son, your dad is brave." In that terrifying experience, surely he didn't feel brave in the midst of it. But afterward, since he did what was hard and scary and needed to be done, he came to know his own character, that he was a man of courage, and got the glory of sharing that fact with his son.

An Introduction to Dori Day

A dear friend of mine who embodies so much of what I've shared in these pages is Dori Day.

"We just moved into this apartment 4 days ago, and the kids are already calling it home!" When Dori told me that, I had to hear more. In that little phrase, Dori debunked all these ideas so many of us may have had about what it takes to create a home. Does it have to be permanent? Nope. Do you have to be there a long time to homestead? Nuh-uh. Does it have to cost a lot? Negative, ghost rider. She created that home on a shoestring budget.

What's interesting is that when Dori and her husband built their own home and moved into it, their kids asked to go back "home" for 7 months before they felt settled in. So if it has taken you longer in the past, take heart! From today, it can come quite quickly if you'd like. Dori wasn't born knowing it either, but she figured it out just like you're doing.

After Dori made that comment, I asked her if she would write down her findings for you all. This is another shortcut for you, so you don't necessarily have to move several times like they did or find it by trial and error. Dori has made a list of the physical items that help her and her family thrive, and she's presented it in a short, simple way that explains why, so that you can apply it to your own life and adjust it based on what matters to you. She also told me, "I feel like whether or not our home thrives depends a lot more on the habits and routines that we have tried to keep." So she connects the physical items to the habits they help facilitate.

One more little story Dori gave me permission to share is the response people have when they come into their apartment. She said people often comment on how "nice" it is. They have space for their shoes by the door, they've gotten rid of the items that aren't needed for their family to thrive, and there's an intentional flow that people pick up on. But here's the secret she shared with me: the couch is broken in more than one place, most of the furnishings are secondhand, and the tablecloth is the finishing piece that keeps the old dining table looking presentable! They have created "home" on their current budget. Sure, they look forward to upgrading to higher-quality pieces when it's the right time for them, but home is more than a dream space and an unlimited budget. How encouraging!

So without further ado, I introduce you to Dori Day. The following is an excerpt written by Dori. I've included it here because it so well reiterates the principles of this book and gives you a different voice to hear them through. Enjoy...

Thriving in Our Home – by Dori Day

To be able to thrive in my home (whatever size it is), the items that I use to furnish it should not only reflect what is important to my family, but should make it easier for us to uphold those values. For example, if sharing family meals is important, then having a central dining table that is big enough for everyone to be around is a must. A table that is too small or a bar that the kids sit up to and directs my husband and I to the sofa won't help us uphold the family value of a connected mealtime, resulting in an area that we are not thriving in. Based upon my family values, here are the essential furniture items for our household to thrive.

Children's Bedrooms

- A bed that looks and feels like a bed.
- Carpet or rug.
- A night stand or small dresser with a lamp.
- A special spot that is only theirs (could be a bin, drawer, or closet shelf).
- An easily accessible place for their clothes that is also easy to keep organized.
- A small bookshelf for the essential books.
- Small bins or an organizer that children can use to keep their own things tidy.

Master Bedroom

- A bed that looks and feels like a bed
- Carpet or a rug.
- A special spot for each grown up that is only theirs (can be his/hers nightstands)
- At least one night stand with a lamp.
- A dresser or closet system that is easily accessible and easy to keep organized.
- A spot for the essential books.

Living Room

- Enough couch/ seating space for our family to be together.
- A cupboard/cabinet/organizer for all the family items to have a spot. (remotes, Gaming console, yoga equipment, games and toys, blankets, etc.)
- Lighting or a lamp that can be dimmed.
- A rug or carpet that makes being on the floor fun.

Dining room

- A table that is big enough to seat our family and is easily accessible for meals

Kitchen

- The basic cooking utensils for making meals. As well as basic pots, pans and baking dishes.
- Enough dishes to get our family through a full day of meals and snacks.
- Small appliances that reflect our family's eating habits (should always have a place they can be put away.) Some staples for me are toaster, blender, coffee maker, 3 in 1 pressure cooker/air fryer/slow cooker, and beater.

Laundry room/space: A place designated for laundry that can be contained, closed off, and put away.

Entrance/ Entry space: A well-defined place for shoes. Another for gloves and hats, a third for coats and backpacks, and a fourth for keys and sunglasses. A shelf with a basket is useful, as are hooks and sticky hooks.

Bathrooms

- Functional bathroom necessities that are easy to keep clean and maintain - shower curtain, rug, towels, hand towels and facial cloths, toilet roll holder, toilet brush and toilet brush set.
- Bathroom hooks for towels and robes.
- A space for hygiene products that can be easily put away after use.

Office Space

- Desk
- Chair
- Lamp
- Shelf/organizer for office supplies, extra chargers, etc.
- Filing system whether physical or digital.

Extra Storage Space: Somewhere to put seasonal gear, decorations, and equipment that is outside of our immediate living space.

Some things that are helpful for me to ask when thinking about bringing new items into our home are:

- Does it meet a need or solve a problem that I have right now?
- Does it bring me closer to meeting my family values?
- At what point in my day am I going to use this? Is it going to be easy to use? Can I visualize the time in my day right now that I would choose to use it over something I am using now?
- How easy will this item be to pull out, assemble, and use? What about ease of cleaning and taking care of it?
- Where will this item belong? If I am looking for it, where will I go to find it? Is there space for it in this place?

When I think of my space and what to put into it, I like to ask if this item will help or hinder me and my family in carrying out our habits and routines that uphold our family values. I got the idea from reading several books on habits, visualization, creating visions, and then setting up your space to help you succeed. "Habit is stronger than reason," so I like to make our space into something I don't have to think about. We just flow through our habits. In this flow state is where my family thrives! I want to spend my mental energy pouring into my family, not trying to navigate my space.

My husband and I value faith, family togetherness, education and learning, and feeling and acting our best. When we visualize what we want our family to look like in 10 years and what kind of adults we want our children to be, we ask, "What is it going to take to get us there?" This gives us a good idea of what our family values should be and the necessary accompanying habits.

Our home furnishings are functional. Those that aren't are meaningful and aim to set a tone that we want in our home. This doesn't exactly make it the most attractive home from an interior design perspective (although we do try to make it look nice because we also enjoy that). But our home is happy! It is a place where we thrive.

Key Points from Dori's Story

Dori's philosophy and effort have helped her create a home for her and her family. Their home is personal by supporting their values. The spaces are functional since they set them up to facilitate order and good habits. There's a simplicity in her clarity and cleanliness. Finally, their spaces are appealing to the eye for them because they value that too, and because the order and declutter is pleasant to behold. How inspiring! You can work towards the same, one little step at a time, and enjoy each small victory along the way.

Creating Lasting Change: How to Not Lose Steam

In general, try taking a 30,000-foot view, as if you were walking into someone else's home or a vacation rental and were not responsible for the 'to do's'. Imagine that you didn't have any plans or ideas for changes or upgrades and just soak up your home as it is today. Let it be both/and instead of either/or; we can both appreciate our home for what it is today and dream of what it will be one day (remembering that even if those changes are a big upgrade, they won't offer what our home today does, so both have a beauty to them).

There is a recipe for home with lots of space for personalization, and like a recipe, we can add ingredients or hold the pepper. We can make it our own. It has the items you need and love and not the ones that don't serve you. It's a reflection of who we are and is personal. It's beautiful to the people living in it. It serves us as we go about our day.

Putting it All in Perspective

This is more than just managing a household. We get to create an atmosphere and an environment. That can be an environment where we can come as we are and feel welcome; an environment that our kids then grow up wanting to create for themselves and their families one day; a place that's happy and homey, that's well-ordered so that it brings clarity, with a simplicity that lets you take a load off and just be. This is an environment that's beautiful to you, soothing to the eye, and that creates an ambiance that feels good to be in. This is a gift to yourself and the world.

If there are aspects of your environment that aren't quite where you want them to be yet, notice them and accept them. Then start the joyful work of bringing them into alignment with where you want them to be on your terms. This is good and holy work, and you can do it.

At the end of the day, at the end of our lives, what have we contributed to the world? Have we brought a place with a little beauty? Have we shared a little peace and hospitality, warmth and love? All of these can ooze out of the walls of our home. They first bless us and then spill over onto neighbor and friend, family and foe. Like a light on a hill, our home can serve as a beacon of hope and a guiding light. Here's to you and your home.

Personal Monthly Budget Template

Use this template to plan your monthly budget with a 10% tithe as the first priority line item.

Income

- Primary Income: $
- Secondary Income: $
- Other Income: $

Total Monthly Income: $

Giving & Generosity

- Tithe (10% of Total Income): $
- Other Giving / Offerings: $

Savings & Investments

- Emergency Fund: $
- Long-Term Savings: $
- Retirement Contributions: $
- Kids' Savings / College Funds: $

Housing

- Mortgage / Rent: $
- Property Taxes (if monthly): $
- Home Insurance: $
- Utilities: $
- Internet: $
- Home Maintenance: $

Transportation

- Car Payment(s): $
- Gas: $
- Insurance: $
- Maintenance / Repairs: $
- Registration: $

Food

- Groceries: $
- Eating Out: $

Health

- Health Insurance: $
- Medical / Dental / Vision: $
- Medications / Supplements: $
- Fitness: $

Personal & Family

- Clothing: $
- Kids' Activities / School Costs: $
- Childcare: $
- Gifts: $
- Subscriptions / Memberships: $

Insurance

- Life Insurance: $
- Other Insurance: $

Debt Payments

- Student Loans: $
- Credit Cards: $
- Other Loans: $

Fun / Lifestyle

- Entertainment: $
- Hobbies: $
- Travel Fund: $

Total Monthly Expenses: $

Remaining Balance: $

(Income minus Total Expenses)

Tip: You can also do this exercise to build an annual budget by looking at 12 months at a time.

Personal Renovation Budget Template

Use this template to estimate and track the cost of your home renovation. It includes holding costs and easily overlooked expenses. Note that for any that don't apply to your project just put $0.

Project Information

- Project Name:
- Property Address:
- Start Date:
- Estimated Completion Date:

Funding Sources

- Cash on Hand: $
- Other Funding: $

Total Available Funding: $

Pre-Construction Costs
- Architectural Plans / Drawings: $
- Engineering Reports: $
- Permits & Permit Fees: $
- City/County Inspections: $
- Surveys / Site Assessments: $
- Appraisal (if financing): $
- Environmental Testing (mold, asbestos, radon): $

Demolition & Site Prep
- Demo Labor: $
- Dumpster / Hauling Fees: $
- Temporary Fencing / Security: $
- Portable Toilet (if needed): $
- Debris Disposal: $
- Site Cleanup (initial): $

Structural & Exterior Work
- Foundation Repairs: $
- Framing: $
- Roofing: $
- Exterior Siding / Repairs: $
- Windows / Exterior Doors: $
- Masonry / Concrete Repairs: $

Mechanical Systems (MEP)
- Electrical Work: $
- Plumbing: $
- HVAC: $
- Water Heater Replacement: $
- Venting / Ductwork: $

Interior Finishes

- Drywall / Texture: $
- Interior Paint: $
- Flooring: $
- Cabinets: $
- Countertops: $
- Trim / Baseboards: $
- Interior Doors & Hardware: $
- Lighting Fixtures: $
- Plumbing Fixtures: $

Kitchen & Bathroom Specific

- Appliances: $
- Kitchen Fixtures / Finishes: $
- Bathroom Fixtures / Finishes: $
- Tile work (floor & shower): $
- Shower Glass: $

Exterior & Yard

- Landscaping: $
- Sprinkler Repairs: $
- Driveway / Concrete: $
- Fencing / Gates: $
- Deck / Patio Work: $

Holding Costs (Often Overlooked)

- Mortgage or Rent During Renovation: $
- Property Taxes: $
- Property Insurance (including Builder's Risk): $
- Utilities (Water, Gas, Electric): $
- HOA Fees: $
- Loan Interest Payments: $

Tip: The key here is to capture extra costs that are not in your normal budget. If the renovations are taking place before you move in, and you're having to pay expenses on a second home during the project, enter those here. If you've moved out and are renting, then simply include the extra rental costs and 20-25% additional utilities if more power is being used while the contractors are working.

Other Overlooked Costs
- Contingency / Unexpected Repairs (10–20%): $
- Tool Rentals / Equipment Rentals: $
- Temporary Storage Unit: $
- Security System or Monitoring: $
- Cleaning (mid-project and final): $
- Delivery Fees for Materials: $
- Fuel / Transportation for Supply Runs: $
- Meals / Convenience Costs During Reno: $

Professional Services
- General Contractor Fees: $
- Designer / Consultant Fees: $
- Project Manager: $
- Specialty Contractors: $

Totals
- Total Estimated Renovation Cost: $
- Remaining Budget: $
  (Available Funding minus Total Renovation Cost)

About the Author

Maya Murphy has completed 20 renovations, alongside her husband, Dave, making homes beautiful and functional without breaking the bank! With a background in management, investing, and stewardship, she brings a practical and thoughtful approach wrapped in a sunny and cheeky demeanor. Their latest renovation—the first one they designed for their own family—left her inspired and feeling called to share what truly turns a house into a home. The experience opened her eyes to the practical, personal, and spiritual layers that make a space grounding, meaningful, and just plain fun. She enjoys adventure, sunshine, and chocolate, especially with Dave and their four kids: Cole, Amora, Mark, and Nicholas.

Acknowledgements

What would I do without y'all? First, thank you to my husband Dave Murphy. You are an irreplaceable part of this. Love, you've believed in me and inspired me to get it done! Thank you for investing in me, in this, and in us. There's no one I'd rather build a home and a life with than you.

To Cole and Amora, you knew this was important, that it would bless people, and that I could do it. You lovingly reminded me when I needed it. You've also taught me how to fill a home with love and to just be present. You sure make life fun and full! Thank you to both of you, and to your siblings Mark and Nicholas, for filling our home with precious memories.

To my friend Rob Marshall, you have been a guiding light. When I got too serious, you called me the "shortest nuclear reactor of sunshine!" You've been a part of this project since it was a nucleus of an idea and have seen it through with me. Thank you for your feedback and support.

To my friend Lindsey Greenawalt, you helped me learn how to clear out the mental and spiritual junk getting in the way of us feeling at home. You anchor me back to God and help me arise. Your guidance is woven into these pages.

To my friend Dori Johnson, you are sunshine! You believe in me and continually remind me of the importance of the work God calls us to do. Iron sharpens iron, and so it is every time we get the opportunity to connect.

You graciously did not let me let go of this calling. You've shown me that the point is joy! Thank you for all you've contributed here and for including your voice in these pages.

Thank you to everyone on the team who helped with launching, editing, inspiring, mentoring, and pictures, especially: Casey Mazure, Anne LeBlanc, Cara Deviny, Krista Allmond, Kira Anderson, Coco Mbassi, Sterling Jaquith, Selma Sierra, Autumn Cook, Colton Mewborne, Mary Dragoset, Tori Cook, Lisa Dragoset, Barbara Rollauer, Nika Huffman, Maria LeBlanc, Amy Loniewsky, Teresa Harke, Teresa Carlson, Grace Carlson. Lilly Carlson, Emma Carlson, Cynthia Hernandez, Kateri Reyes, Cheryl Gallegos, Alyssa Harrington, Rebecca Dussault, Jordan Ring-Sakabe, Yuki Ring-Sakabe, Allie Canaday, Kinga Szewczyk, Kateri Reyes, Amanda Maxwell, Elsa Delepine, Marla Cota, Andy Berven, Kurt Bubna, Katelynn Koontz, and Dandy Anwuacha. And last but not least, thank you to the Holy Spirit!

Urgent Plea

Thanks For Reading My Home Book!

I love hearing what you have to say and appreciate all your feedback.

Your input helps other readers *and* helps me make future books even better. No fancy words needed—just a few thoughts from the heart.

👉 Please share **two minutes** now to leave a quick Amazon review, perhaps while you sip a warm drink.

Thank you truly,

~ *Maya Murphy*

www.ingramcontent.com/pod-product-compliance
Lightning Source LLC
Chambersburg PA
CBHW051522150726
47997CB00001B/345